NATALIE AND NAOMI EVANS

Natalie and Naomi Evans are the founders of the anti-racism platform @everydayracism_, which has over 200k followers on Instagram. They share stories from BIPOC and educational posts focusing on how to be anti-racist, provide anti-racism sessions for organisations such as Bupa and Lloyds Bank and write articles for *Red*, *Grazia* and more. Their work has been featured in the *i* newspaper and they recently appeared on the Channel 5 news documentary *Everyday Racism*.

Naomi and Natalie are committed to empowering people to make a difference in the world. They are natural communicators who believe education and action are the fundamental route to stopping social injustice. Their aim is to help dismantle systemic racism by empowering BIPOC and teaching white people how to use their privilege for change.

T0332963

NATALIE AND NAOMI EVANS

The Mixed-Race Experience

Reflections and Revelations
on Multicultural Identity

VINTAGE

1 3 5 7 9 10 8 6 4 2

Vintage is part of the Penguin Random House group of companies
whose addresses can be found at global.penguinrandomhouse.com

First published in Vintage in 2023
First published in hardback by Square Peg in 2022

Copyright © Natalie and Naomi Evans 2022

Natalie and Naomi Evans have asserted their right to be identified
as the authors of this Work in accordance with the Copyright,
Designs and Patents Act 1988

penguin.co.uk/vintage

Printed and bound in Great Britain by Clays Ltd, Elcograf S.p.A.

The authorised representative in the EEA is Penguin Random House Ireland,
Morrison Chambers, 32 Nassau Street, Dublin D02 YH68

A CIP catalogue record for this book is available from the British Library

ISBN 9781529115031

Penguin Random House is committed to a sustainable future
for our business, our readers and our planet. This book is made
from Forest Stewardship Council® certified paper.

*To the mixed-race folk who have been
searching for a place to belong.*

Contents

CONTENTS

Introduction

The distinct memory of Saturday mornings in our family home. The smell of Dad's Softsheen Magic shaving powder pinching the backs of our throats. The sound of bacon and eggs sizzling in the pan downstairs from Mum making breakfast. The vibrations from the record player belting out Bob Marley's 'Three Little Birds' so loud it woke us up and called us downstairs. 'Come here, your hair needs combing out!' Dad would say, looking at our thick, brown, dry mass of curls. We would look at each other and charge back upstairs, laughing. When Dad brushed out our hair, it hurt. 'Leave them alone!' Mum would say. She didn't see the problem with letting our hair run free, but Dad didn't like it. For us, growing up in a mixed-race family sometimes felt like occupying the space in between. Not always knowing which way to turn, which parent to listen to. Often trying to navigate who we were and who we wanted to be.

This is the book that we wish we had when we were growing up. The book we would have wanted our parents to read and the book we wish we could have given to our family and friends to help them better understand some of the experiences we would have, and issues that we would face. It's complex. No one's life episodes are identical. There is no singular, 'mixed-race experience', but one thing we've learned through writing this book is that – as with any community of people – there are distinct commonalities and threads that link us.

You may or may not identify as mixed race. We hope that those of you reading this who do not identify as mixed race will find something new to reflect upon. Perhaps you are in an interracial relationship, or raising mixed-race children, or maybe you are simply intrigued to learn more about something unfamiliar to you. Whatever has brought this book to you, we hope you will read with an open heart and mind. Whenever you bring people together – whether it's discussing experiences of class, race, gender or sexuality – there must be room for listening to, and learning from, each other. We have written with reference to our own lives and have also interviewed a range of people, reflecting different facets of the mixed-race experience. We are immensely grateful to everyone who gave up their time and opened up to us, sharing their thoughts and reflections, so we could share people's stories and insights with you at this moment in our time.

This book will, inevitably, have its limitations. For one, the title itself implies there is one account to be told, which is, of course, not the case. We are from a small seaside town in England. The area we grew up in was white-majority, and it wasn't until we moved away that we realised just how problematic some situations in our childhood had been. We have one white and one Black parent. As mixed-race women racialised as Black, we face racism and sexism and, at the same time, hold other privileges such as being light-skinned, able-bodied and cisgender. We will never experience homophobia, transphobia or ableism.

Mixed-race people are not a homogenous group. We would never be able to write a neat little book about such a wealth of identities and nor would we want to. Being mixed race is often depicted as having at least one white parent and one Black parent, but this, too, is a misconception. We would not try to, and would never want to, write on behalf of others, which is why we interviewed a range of people and have included their quotes and stories to try to reflect the subjects that can arise within the mixed-race experience. We do not for one moment suggest that we have covered everything, but we have aimed to cover some of the main congruities within the experiences of a selection of people who identify as belonging to a mixed-race community – congruities such as colourism, racism and identity, to name a few.

This book doesn't hold all the answers, and it is certainly not the end of the conversation – it's a starting point. We present stories, guidance and support for those exploring their identities through the complexities of this world. Many of the themes and issues that arise can also apply to other aspects of our identity because, we believe, many of us are looking to understand ourselves better and find a place to belong. One of the most interesting things we discovered on the journey of writing was, while our focus was primarily on a particular group of people, many of the issues and parallels were concerned with how it feels to navigate life as a non-white person, and the impact of feeling like you don't belong. The sense that you are 'other', haven't found your community or feel rejected is incredibly destabilising, though we know that these feelings and experiences are not exclusive to those who identify as mixed race.

We hope our writing will provoke further learning and perhaps begin some conversations for you and your closer circles that may have never been had. Perhaps it will help you feel more confident in how you identify. We hope it will give you a better understanding of the beauty and complexities mixed-race people are sometimes not able to express openly. We hope you will read this and know the mixed-race identity – in all its facets – is valid. We hope that if you are mixed race, you finish this book knowing you are enough with no side to choose.

Naomi and Natalie xx

Why 'Mixed Race'?

The term 'mixed race' certainly has its limitations and there will be those of you reading this book who will consciously choose not to use it. You may find the term problematic because race is a social construct[1] and to use the term 'mixed race' implies that race is based on biological attributes. Using it could be considered as reinforcing an idea of race as based on fact. We opted to use the term because it is how we have always identified and how we currently feel most comfortable. It was also important to us to dispel the idea that being mixed race includes only two ancestral groups, which is implied in the term 'dual heritage' (and which is so often considered a mix of Black and white). Some people will choose the term 'biracial' or 'multiracial'. We also recognise that this may change. The term 'mixed' can also be dubious in that it can evoke negative connotations, such as being 'confused', 'mixed up' or 'unbalanced'. This has often been peddled through the age-old literary trope of the 'tragic mulatto', which dates to the nineteenth century, and in which light-skinned, mixed-race characters are represented either as suicidal upon discovering their ancestry or as sexually seductive – essentially, born to be hurt and/or to cause harm. Then there will, of course, be some mixed-race people who will choose to identify monoracially. We encourage you to explore language and how you identify until you feel comfortable. This may also change over time. The bottom line is it is your choice as to how you identify, and not for anyone else to tell you how.

"Why Mixed Race?"

Chapter 1

Everyday Racism:

On growing up in a white-majority area

~~~

Natalie: In October 2019 I stepped off the train at my home station of Margate, a small seaside town about an hour away from London. My hands were shaking, adrenalin was pumping and tears were rolling down my face. I took my phone out of my bag and called my sister, Naomi. I had no way of knowing at the time that the incident I had witnessed and filmed would change the trajectory of both our lives.

It was a cold Friday afternoon. I had finished a day of back-to-back meetings in London and was feeling sick from the endless cups of coffee I'd downed to sustain me through the many dull conversations I had endured that day. I'd missed the direct train home, so I had to change stations halfway. I stood on the platform, thinking about whether I should listen to a podcast or finish watching the programme I'd downloaded the night before. As I wrestled with this very important decision I watched my train arrive through the tunnel. Stepping into the carriage, I noticed it was full. Glancing around, I observed that all the passengers were white. I find you pick up on these things when you are used to being the minority in the room – something I find white people in this country can often take for granted. I remember once my mum rolling her eyes when one of my dad's friends returned from a holiday in Jamaica and commented to her on how he had gone to a football match and was one of the only white guys there. 'Yes, well,' she replied, flatly, 'imagine how it was for George growing up here.' Mum would often have to challenge ignorant comments like this.

I sat down on one of the few available seats, rested my bag on my lap, turned my podcast on, put my headphones in, leaned back and closed my eyes. It swiftly hit me how tired I was at that moment. As the train pulled into the next stop, I heard the faint noise of doors beeping, and heard (what I assumed) to be two men getting on the train. They were being extremely loud. I opened my eyes as the men walked past and sat down on the seats in front of me. Looking through the gap in the seats, I could see they were each holding a can of beer. The two men were white, looked to be in their late twenties and sipped their beers, all the while talking loudly to each other, as though they were the only ones on the train. I observed passengers around me shuffling and looking around to see who was making so much noise.

I closed my eyes again, turned my podcast up and ignored them, hoping they would be getting off at the next stop. It was then that I heard another voice coming from behind me. This time, it was the train conductor. 'Tickets please,' he called out. I sat up, shuffled around for the small piece of card I had shoved into my wallet and held it in my hand, ready for when he approached. I paused my podcast and as I looked up, he gave me 'The Nod'. I nodded back. For those of you that don't know about 'The Nod', it's a common code in the Black community, especially when you're in white spaces. Musa Okwonga refers to it as 'a swift, yet intimate statement of ethnic solidarity . . . [a way of saying] "Wow, well, I really didn't expect to see another one of us out here, but you seem to be doing your thing just fine. More power to you, and all the very best."'[1] Growing up, I would watch my dad give 'The Nod' to other Black men and women, thinking at the time he had a lot of friends!

I handed the conductor my ticket, and he thanked me and continued on his way. It was at that moment I looked over at the two loud, beer-drinking men and I knew in my gut not to turn my podcast back on. The train conductor approached them and said, 'Tickets please,' but there was no reply. 'Tickets please,' he repeated, as though unsure whether or not they'd heard him. Again, there was complete silence. He asked a third time, his voice louder and more abrupt than before. One of the men turned to look up at the train conductor and, in full earshot of the other passengers, said, 'I ain't got a ticket, mate,' before turning away, smirking.

The train conductor replied, 'Well, you need a ticket before you get on the train.'

With a big sigh, as if the train conductor was a huge inconvenience, the white man turned again and said, 'I am getting off at the next stop, mate, so I don't need a ticket.'

'That's not true,' the train conductor responded, in a calm manner. 'Everyone needs a ticket before they get on the train, even if it's only one stop.'

My heart started beating faster. I had a gut feeling that this was going to turn ugly, and I was right. The white man shouted, 'Well, did you get a fucking passport to get into the fucking country?' I was immediately filled with rage, but, unsure how to help, I did the only thing I felt I could in that moment: I pulled my phone out and pressed 'record'.

As the racist altercation continued, I looked around the carriage to see how others had responded. There was a woman pretending to scroll through her phone; a couple who promptly rose to move seats; a man shaking his head, but saying nothing and two young boys watching like this was a wrestling match. I knew one thing for sure: not one person was going to say anything. I continued to record. The longer it went on, the more infuriated I became, watching the conductor trying to negotiate with the men. 'Why would you ask if I have a passport?' the conductor continued. 'Are you asking me because I am Black?'

9

One of the men responded, 'I've got two mixed-race kids and [the conductor] thinks I'm racist . . . it's always the Black card, innit?' The train conductor sighed, turned and walked away in the same direction he came from back through the carriage. As he walked past me I could see a defeated look on his face. It was then that I stood up, and the rest is a bit of a blur.

I've since watched the footage of me confronting the men, but it always feels like it was someone else speaking. The recording also serves as my only memory of the incident, because my mind remains completely blank. 'Are you joking?' I said.

'What?' said the white guy.

I continued, 'What you said is racist. And your children . . . poor them, if their dad is going to speak like that!' I knew what I had said didn't exactly make sense, but it was all I could muster together.

'Yeah but . . .' he scrambled.

'No,' I interrupted. 'What you said was racist.' My voice was still shaking, but firm. 'Would you have said that if he was white? What does having a passport got to do with your train ticket?' My phone was still recording.

'Well, when I went to Ireland . . .' the guy started, while the other man sat there, mute.

I cut in. 'That's not what I am asking you. What has a passport got to do with your train ticket? You need a ticket like everyone else,' I repeated. The man had no answer; he had nothing. He sprang out of his seat. *Here we go*, I thought, *he is going to attack me now.* I'd called him out for being racist, and as a woman, I am also all too familiar with toxic masculinity. In the past, I've noted that when a man's ego is bruised, he can become aggressive. To my surprise, he walked past me and shouted after the conductor, 'Mate, I am sorry. I am sorry.' The conductor turned round, shook his head, and walked away.

I couldn't quite believe what I'd said had had an effect. I didn't handle it perfectly, and said some things that didn't make sense, but it still seemed to have made a difference. I decided to move carriages because I didn't want to be near the men anymore, and I spent the rest of the journey feeling physically sick. As I made my way through the carriage, I could see people staring at me. Some gave me a smile, as if to say, 'Well done.' Others looked at me as if I was the one making trouble and had disturbed their peaceful train journey home. I was sure they were thinking, *She should have kept out of it.*

As I sat down, the train stopped and I saw the two men get off, still holding their cans of beer. Relief ran through my body, but I wanted to see the train conductor and check he was OK. I have experienced racism so much in my own life and I know what the feeling is like when it's done so publicly and there is nowhere to go. Fortunately, he walked by again. We chatted; he was visibly upset. I forwarded the video footage to the conductor – never to see each other again.*

The rest of the journey felt like forever. When the train finally pulled into my station, I stepped onto the platform and called Naomi straight

---

*I did see the conductor again at the end of 2021. I was on the train heading to London from Margate and when I looked up, he was walking towards me asking to see train tickets. When I asked him if his name was [. . .] he looked concerned, he didn't understand how I knew him. Then when I explained he smiled. We chatted. I asked to take a picture and he politely asked me not to put it on social media. He told me how he also got a lot of attention from that video. It was lovely to see him again as I think about him often.

away. I needed to speak to someone who would understand. I told her everything, and we both asked each other the same question we have asked ourselves our whole lives:

'Why did nobody else say anything?'

There began the desire to speak our truth and start sharing publicly how racism shows up for people every day. After much deliberation, six months later, I shared the video on social media, and it went viral. The outpouring – both of solidarity and ignorance – led to the idea that people should have the space to share their truth and give practical advice. It was then that our Instagram account @everydayracism_ was born.

Challenging racism is nothing new to us. We grew up in a white-majority town, with a white mum, white teachers, white postman, white church leaders, white gym instructors, white doctors and white friends. We were often the only mixed-race women in our spaces and there were only a handful of non-white students in the schools we attended. We were never taught by any Black teachers. We went to parties where people thought it was acceptable to do blackface. Our hair was openly fondled. We were often in positions where we had to challenge racism and were rarely backed up. It was a town where the British National Party (BNP) would come and march, and the United Kingdom Independence Party (UKIP) leader Nigel Farage felt confident he could be elected as a member of parliament. When we wrote to our local MP, Roger Gale, about our concerns with racism in the area, he confidently informed us that our fears were unfounded – he had an excellent working relationship with all of the 'ethnic and faith groups' in east Kent.

Growing up in our small seaside town, the only other groups of Black people we would see were day-trippers who would visit by coach from London. As we walked along the seafront, our eyes would literally light up when we saw people who looked like us. The longing to be noticed and to have a group of people who would understand, rather than mock our heritage, was something we craved. It was only when we were much older that we realised how deeply damaging that void had been. However, as we grew up and gravitated towards what we characterised as our 'Blackness', we began to realise that what we craved couldn't be found there either. Understanding more about our Jamaican culture and heritage was, of course, essential, but it still left the unanswered question: 'What is *my* identity?'

Spending time with our Black family – whether it was travelling to London or Nottingham to see cousins and aunties or flying over to Jamaica to stay with our dad – never satisfied that sense of needing to belong. Even though it taught us so many positive things and we were lucky enough to be able to travel, we also didn't feel fully at ease in those spaces either. We would feel we weren't Black enough, but we also knew we weren't white, so this pain of not feeling enough of anything grew progressively stronger and stronger. It was like carrying around this sense of guilt and shame for only being half of what the world named us as. This wasn't anyone's fault; we generally had a good relationship with both sides of our family and our mum tried her hardest to ensure that we were connected to our identity. She tried to help us understand our heritage. She took us to Jamaica once a year and our dad – who by this time had moved back to his hometown of Montego Bay – would also come and visit us in the UK. She made friends with other Black families who lived in the area and sought out hairdressers and hair products. She tried to cook Jamaican food for us. One Christmas, she dressed up a Black Barbie doll and put it on top of the Christmas tree because there were no Black or brown angels in the shops at the time. She tried, but no matter how hard you try, growing up as a non-white person in a white-majority town is always going to be hard. Whiteness is the default. When it comes to trust, success, and beauty standards, it is whiteness. When we became teenagers, there was generally only one thing that was important to us and that was to be liked, accepted and to fit in. With our 'unruly' curly Afro hair and brown skin, it seemed impossible to not stand out.

Our mum, Penelope (she/her), is white British and in her mid-sixties. She shared what it was like raising us in a white-majority town:

Mum: It was a big learning curve for me. When I first had Naomi, it was 1983. I remember a nurse coming into my room at the hospital and saying, 'Oh, she's very dark; is her father dark?' and I said, 'Yes he is.' When he walked in, there was like this [strange] look on her face, and I got that a few times with the nurses. I think the first time it really hit me was when Naomi was a very new baby in the pram, and I was taking her for a walk. An older lady came up and said, 'Oh, can I look at your baby?' She looked in the pram, turned to me with this look on her face and said, 'Never mind; she will probably get lighter as she gets older.' I was stunned. I never said anything to her. I couldn't believe what I'd heard. Then after that I would have people say things like, 'Oh, brown babies are always really attractive,' and I noticed people fetishising mixed-race babies, and it was so uncomfortable.

Naomi and Natalie: How were the school years for you, and watching us grow up in a white-majority town?

Mum: It was tricky. There were times when I did make a fuss and I had no qualms about it whatsoever, and other times where I'd think, should I just keep quiet? I didn't want to make it worse for you. Naomi was born in 1983, Natalie in 1989 and Rachel in 1997 and there were quite a lot of years' difference and changes over that time. When Naomi started school, it was very different and basically, if you were non-white, you were grouped all into one. I remember a few racist incidents that happened to all of you in school, including incidents to do with your hair. Even now, people feel they can touch a Black person's hair. I even have it with the grandchildren when I take them out.

You each had your own hair journeys. Naomi went through a lot to try and feel comfortable with her hair. I was not experienced with Black hair and I had a lot to learn. It was helpful that your father's aunt and cousins helped; we would travel to Nottingham and London because you couldn't get Black hair products where we lived. I sometimes got them sent from America, along with Black Barbie dolls. I really did try and source things that were relevant for you, including magazines, if I could, because there was nothing – there were no Black references for you growing up.

Naomi and Natalie: Did you ever feel that you needed to have a conversation about race with us all?

Mum: No, I don't think I did. Oh, that feels terrible now. I think I was always open to acknowledging it with you and supporting you and, if necessary, saying something at school or to people. I didn't ignore it. I certainly like to feel that you could say anything to me. I can remember when you [Natalie] started going on the bus on your own and you came back [one day], and you were so upset. When I asked why you said this woman at the bus stop kept asking, 'Where do you come from?' and you said 'Margate.' She said 'No, where do you *really* come from?' and you got upset because she kept asking you. I remember explaining to you that she was referring to your heritage and she shouldn't have been questioning you like that. I remember one day after you started primary school, you said, 'Mum, tie my hair up as tight as you can. I don't want any bits out. The dinner ladies keep touching it and saying it feels like candy floss.' It was a real shame.

Naomi and Natalie: What about Rachel [our younger sister] and helping her to understand a bit more about her heritage and her experience growing up in a white-majority town?

Mum: When I adopted Rachel, I did ask questions about her being Ghanaian and was there anything I needed to know? I was told historically that Jamaican heritage was often linked to Ghana, so there was likely to be some historical link. However, I was also aware that Ghana is different to Jamaica. We were fortunate in that within the church we went to at the time, we had Ghanaian friends, so I felt that we could make links there. Rachel came from a background where she had no Black references at all. For her to come and live with us – to have two sisters who were also mixed race – I thought [it] was a great thing. She was brought up from quite a young age with a white foster family who had absolutely no idea at all about how to raise Black children, about their needs or identity. [Rachel] was in a school with no other Black children, and she was having a very difficult time there. I remember when I first met her; I went to see her with Naomi. I took a craft activity to do, and we were sitting around the table. While we were doing this craft, she gave a side look to Naomi and said, 'I can't read, you know. I'm stupid because I'm brown.'

Naomi said, 'Well, that's a load of rubbish. I am brown and I'm not stupid.' Rachel had associated the fact that she couldn't read with the fact that she was brown. I went and met her teacher and I told this to her teacher, who was really defensive and said, 'Well no one has said that to her.' I said, 'Well, no one has *had* to say it to her. That was her own interpretation of her situation.' This was quite something to work with, and she did learn to read the first few weeks she came to live with us.

Sarah Lotus Garrett (she/her) is a life coach and founder of Mixed Bloom Room, a coaching practice that serves mixed people* and their families. She is in her fifties, was born in the US and now lives in Italy. She identifies as mixed Black, and is of African American and East Coast white heritage.

Naomi and Natalie: Can you tell us a bit about growing up and about your family background, i.e. who you grew up with? Where did you grow up and what was that like?

Sarah: I was born in San Francisco in 1969, which was the epicentre of the hippie movement, with a lot of Black Power and political activism going on, but I grew up in Marin County, and in whiteness. I grew up with my mum, who is white. My parents separated when I was about two and my dad moved back to Chicago. Along with my mum, I grew up with my grandparents, who spent a lot of time with me and my brother. I have an older brother who looks like me and, thankfully, we were very close. I think that made a huge difference for me growing up, having that physical affirmation.

My mum remarried when I was ten, and my sister was born shortly after. She's also mixed. I grew up in a place that was super-hippie, super-liberal – nobody would ever admit to being racist. I had a lot of white people, including family members, around me who would say, 'Oh, you have such beautiful brown skin,' but never in the context of the reality of what it is to have brown skin. You know, it was always, 'Oh, I wish I had skin like you,' and then that was it. There was no conversation about the reality of what that was like for me. I think that was probably one of the most profoundly disturbing aspects of my

---

* Sarah uses the term 'mixed people' in her work, and we have retained the use of the term here.

childhood . . . this sort of delusion of liberalism and progressiveness and open-mindedness, and zero space or acknowledgement of race, or my experience or that I was different. Yeah, it was a weird and extremely isolating thing to grow up being so incredibly different and have no space to talk about or explore that.

Naomi and Natalie: Is that because people were the kind of people who said, 'We're not racist. We're pretty liberal,' and so that meant they thought things were OK?

Sarah: Yeah. I also grew up in a place where the people who were 'racist', were *really* racist. There was this time I went to a party when I was younger and around a campfire, one of the kids brought out his dad's white KKK [Klu Klux Klan] hood and waved it around to scare people. They were white hood racists. So, there were extreme racists juxtaposed [with] hippies with a mindset of, 'I have the most open mind in the world and I'm certainly not one of "those racists".' When that happened, I never told my mum about it. That was something I managed on my own. There was no space to tell anybody about that. I think I basically shut down. I just went inside [myself]. I literally put my whole identity in terms of race in a 'disappear' box and I didn't touch it for decades. One thing I did when I was around thirteen was what I would now call 'internalised fetishisation', although it's a bit more nuanced than that. I started wearing a lot of makeup and doing my hair meticulously. I would wake up very early every morning and essentially don a mask. I put all my emphasis on being beautiful and that helped me to be almost invisible racially in the very racially hostile environment where I grew up. Essentially, my beauty upstaged my race, sometimes. I think this is probably a common theme for mixed people. I want to say it's like a mixed fallback, and for me I couldn't ever emulate whiteness because of my skin tone and features, so this was a way to create a buffer between myself and racist people and their actions. My 'beauty' was like a protection. And so, I relied on it intensely when I was younger and into my twenties, even though I've always known that beauty, in the end, is meaningless. Still, I would put a mask on almost every day before going out. And because of colourism, featurism and texturism I was in a privileged position that allowed me more peace and safety than a darker-skinned person would have been afforded. Looking back, I can see how much colourism has protected me, and it's one of the reasons I explore and unpack it within myself and talk about it a lot in my work.

Naomi and Natalie: At what point did you have more realisation of what was going on? Was there anything that happened or was it a kind of growing realisation as time went on?

Sarah: Actually, I think that I needed to leave my country. I didn't leave my country until I was thirty-five. When I left, because my beauty was so far from the standard, that just stopped being a factor and so I was able to let my mask go and just be myself. The racism over here is not like it is in the States. It's not as violent, where [over there] anything can happen anywhere, at any time. We are not always in danger over here. Then I had kids. My son is mixed; he's not dark-skinned, and he holds a lot of light-skinned privilege, but he was still dealing with racist stuff at school. So, it wasn't until much later in my adulthood when he started dealing with racism at school [that] I had to get my shit together quickly, to protect him. I learned the language of white supremacy and whiteness and what it means to be oppressed. I started studying and growing so that I could protect my kids and myself from all the microaggressions, violence and gaslighting of white supremacy. It's fascinating because with racism, once the language comes, you realise that you've known exactly what's been happening all along, you just didn't have a way to language it. It's just like, 'Oh, *that's* what you call that.' From there, it was then an exponential learning about me and the world. Being in Italy has given me more space to explore all this than if I'd been back in the US. Being in a place where I don't speak the language fluently gives me a nice little buffer too. I'm not available to everybody, and so entitled whiteness doesn't have full access to me. I appreciate that.

I do want to tell you about something that I think is super interesting, which occurred when I moved to Italy. It was many years before I realised that the racism that I was dealing with here in Italy was completely different from [the racism] back in the States. I had taken America's racism and brought it here with me, to Italy. Every interaction that I had, I was running on the assumption that I was dealing with American racism and it's not like that at all. I had to ask my husband what Italian racism looks like because I honestly didn't know, and that was a fascinating and incredibly sad realisation: that we – all Americans – bring American racism with us wherever we go.

Naomi and Natalie: Have you got any examples of what racism would look like for you in Italy, compared to America?

Sarah: There's just not a complete and total disregard for human life. Not so much blood in the soil. Italians have white supremacy of their own, but it's not as brutal and violent and unrelenting as American white supremacy. I still have a lot of privilege here as well, you know, especially because I'm American, which Italians apparently still think is cool. I don't know why, but they do. Before they know that I'm American, Italians assume that I am from South America, like Brazil or something, and I came over here to steal an Italian man – ha! If I were dark-skinned and my curls were tighter and if I looked African, they would think, *Oh, she's an immigrant, she comes from a very poor place. She's totally disadvantaged.* So, my experience is incredibly different from somebody who is from, say, Nigeria. Honestly, it's all just variations of the same hideous theme with things being worse for some people because of additional marginalisation, for example, colourism. Which is why our own individual healing for the collective is so important to me. It's why I founded Mixed Bloom Room.

~~~

Natalie: Growing up in white-majority towns when you are racialised as Black or as a Person of Colour is a unique experience. You find yourself in shocking and unfathomable situations, and it's only when you speak about your experiences out loud or confide in someone who grew up in a much more multicultural area that you realise how problematic your upbringing was/is. We're not saying that if you live in a multicultural area, you won't experience any racism, microaggressions or awkward situations because, of course, this is not the case. However, growing up as the significant minority can often mean there are fewer people who recognise situations as problematic, and you can often end up being isolated or exhausted by having to continuously explain things so much so you give up trying.

When I was at secondary school, I was chosen to be in the school production. I must have been about thirteen years old. I couldn't believe it – *me*, being picked to read a poem! I was so proud of myself. I had no idea what the performance was even about and didn't care. I was so happy to be asked. I guess I was a little naive because I was only in Year 8 and had not performed in front of any teachers, so how would they even know if I was going to be OK to read a poem aloud? Rehearsals were after school, and when the bell rang, I grabbed my bag and ran down the corridor to the hall. I was so excited to see what performance I was going to be a part of. As I sat there, surrounded by other students from all different year groups, it was impossible to forget that I was the only mixed-race person in the room – everyone else was white. This may not seem like a big deal, but as a teen, all I wanted to do was blend in. In among the sea of faces I became hyper-aware of how different I looked to my peers. I shuffled in my seat, trying to make myself smaller. As the drama teacher walked in, she announced the name of the show: *Black and White*. Interesting, I thought. I wonder what this is about? Weeks went by and I learned my poem like a good student. The play had lots of different dance routines to songs like 'Black or White' by Michael Jackson. I watched it in awe, thinking one day I could do a dance routine like that. I hadn't told my mum what I was doing for the performance, as I wanted it to be a surprise. Fast-forward to the show – it was my time to shine. As I stood at the side of the stage, I heard a round of applause for the act before me, signalling that it was my turn. The stage lights went down; I walked out with my heart beating fast, my hands shaking and what felt like a frog in my throat. The spotlight came on. I took a deep breath and recited my poem:

They call me Blackie, they call me P***, but I know it's not true,
Because underneath the skin, I am just like you.
They pick on me, they spit on me; I even have no friends,
Sometimes I wonder when will this nightmare ever end?

The poem ended. I heard my applause; the lights went off. *I did it*, I thought. *I remembered all my lines*. At the end of the show we all went back on stage for the final song, 'Melting Pot' by Blue Mink, which was full of racist slurs.

I sang my heart out with pride, and as we finished, we received a standing ovation. As I left the changing room, I couldn't wait to find my mum and sister. Naomi gave me a big hug and told me I did a great job. Mum did the same, but her praise felt a little less sincere. There was something not quite right. Was she disappointed in me? Had I done something wrong? The following week, my mum was at the school visiting my drama teacher. It was only then I realised how controversial this production was. Mum sat me down and explained it all to me. Why the song was racist and why the poem – written by goodness knows who – was othering. This was a performance for white people, centred around whiteness, with terms such as 'I am not like you' – as if there was something wrong with that – and then making me read out racist rhetoric as a 'performance'. My mum went on to further explain to me about white supremacy and ways it shows up. I couldn't believe it. How could I have been so foolish? Only then did it dawn on me why I was even chosen for the show. Of course, a show about being Black and white with an all-white cast doesn't look good. I was their 'token' Black girl. I felt used. Is this how it's going to be? Would I be rolled out whenever they needed me?

As well as this performance, my secondary school experience coincided with the proliferation of 'Girl Power' as the Spice Girls came on the scene. I was immediately dubbed the Mel B lookalike. Not that we did look alike, but the fact that we both identified as female, had brown skin and curly hair was enough to earn me my new nickname. Mel B was like a double-edged sword for me. I liked finally having someone in the spotlight that I could look up to, but being consistently compared to someone purely based on skin colour became frustrating. I remember going to drama school one summer and being in a production of *Cinderella*. Somehow, I ended up being made to play the role of 'Scary Spice'. On reflection, Mel B being the only Black woman in the group, wearing leopard print and being referred to as 'Scary Spice', is highly problematic.

Moving into my later teenage years, I learned how to be 'palatable' for my peers. I would relax my hair to stop other kids from touching it and tell my classmates that Bob Marley was my uncle for kudos. My friends constantly told me how they wanted mixed-race babies when they grew up. My initial interpretation of that was flattery. I felt honoured that they would want their children to look like me.

Even though I did not feel as though I fit into the Black community, I was treated as a Black girl in my school. I allowed white people and businesses to use me to look inclusive. I ticked the ethnicity box for their funding. I was used as the diverse face of events or promo videos and I enjoyed it.

When I was twenty-one, I moved to Jamaica to work and live with my dad. I was treated very differently. I really did think I would feel a sense of belonging there, finally being around Black people, and because I was considered Black growing up, I believed there was no reason why I wouldn't fit in. But it was the opposite. I was the 'browning' – a term that refers to being mixed race or light-skinned in Jamaica – which meant I received a lot of attention and like my upbringing with my white peers, I also stood out. I struggled to understand Jamaican Patois, which made me feel insecure. The culture was completely different to what I was used to; and I didn't know how to meet new people. There were some really positive aspects to living in Jamaica, but at times, it was a lonely and isolating experience. I realised that I had spent a lot of my life feeling othered.

What is 'othering'?

To be 'othered' is to be constantly reminded of your difference from the majority, or excluded from a group due to having characteristics that deviate from what is considered to be the norm.[2] Othering presents itself in many forms, such as touching someone's hair out of curiosity, fetishism, tokenism or violence. However it presents, othering is often tied to power, since the process consistently dehumanises and diminishes one group while simultaneously elevating another. Therefore, being othered can create not only a sense of alienation, but also inferiority and anxiety in those who repeatedly fail to 'fit in'. To combat this, individuals may attempt to modify themselves or assimilate to gain acceptance. Although adaptation is frequently employed by minority groups to navigate instances of othering, a hidden consequence of this process is the internal othering that takes place, presenting as self-hate, internalised racism, anti-Blackness and so on.

Sophie (she/her) is in her mid-thirties and is a singer, music producer and mother of one based in England. She shared with us some of her experiences of growing up mixed race.

Naomi and Natalie: How do you identify, in terms of race?

Sophie: I identify as mixed race. My mother is Scottish and Chinese, and my father is English and Iranian.

Naomi and Natalie: Has there been anything that has influenced you in shaping your racial identity?

Sophie: My mother and my nana have been big influences in terms of embracing having a mixed heritage. My mum and her sister were the only non-white children in their town, and my nana spoke very little English. As a family, they had to deal with a huge amount of racism and adversity and for me, growing up seeing how proud they were of being Chinese and [of] their culture had such a big impact. My siblings and I were constantly reminded in such a positive way that we were Chinese/mixed race.

Naomi and Natalie: Have you ever experienced any microaggressions related to your racial identity?

Sophie: The classic, 'Where are you from? No, I mean where are you *actually* from?' seemed to always be close to the top of the list of questions when I would first meet someone. 'You don't look English', 'You look exotic', and then the game of guessing just 'what' I actually am. When I worked as a waitress in London, I had a man look at me with open-mouthed shock when I spoke to him because, 'Wow, I didn't expect you to have an English accent because you look foreign and you're a waitress!' Another man asked me, 'So, what boat did you come in on?'

~

Naomi: Growing up with brown skin in a white-majority area meant I felt more comfortable in the company of other Black and brown people, but hanging out with Black and brown people wasn't something I had the opportunity to do very often. In what I can only describe as an attempt to fit in to my environment and to feel safe, I spent my childhood and teenage years trying to become as close to what I thought whiteness was. To me, whiteness meant success and opportunity. Racism, Eurocentric ideals of appearance and very little representation of people who looked like me in my upbringing meant I often had negative perceptions of what Blackness was, and I associated this with derogatory connotations, such as poverty, lack of education and crime. As well as being a false narrative, there were three major issues with this line of thinking. First, it meant I was complicit in upholding white supremacy. Second, to white people, I was racialised as Black and, third, I was harbouring internalised anti-Black racism. I lived in a constant state of destabilisation. I would go from wanting to braid my hair and attempting to speak Jamaican Patois to constantly traumatising my hair with heat to get it straight, cutting it into a bob and wearing Barbour jackets to try to emulate my noughties icon, Alexa Chung. At times I relished being different, but I also longed to fit in. In short, I was extremely confused, seeking to find my identity and wanting to feel accepted. I loved my dad, but frankly, there were times – particularly as a young teenager – when I felt embarrassed that when we were all together, we didn't look like the other families around us. I felt the stigmas and assumptions applied to us as soon as we stepped into the room, and it made me incredibly self-conscious.

As I got older, I mastered the art of code-switching. I was desperate to fit in and be the 'good Black girl', even carrying with me some wild notions that if white people could like me or be friends with me, they wouldn't be racist to other people. It was a pressure I had put on myself, yet I was completely oblivious to what I was carrying. When I was with my white friends and colleagues, I dressed and spoke in a particular way to feel as though I fit in. I had a real love for drama and theatre growing up, and a brilliant teacher who did lots of elocution exercises with us, so I was often told I was 'well spoken and articulate'. I took this as a compliment and utilised it to gain social capital. I had also travelled to Jamaica and Kenya on numerous occasions in my teenage years, so by the time I went to university, I could retell stories about my heritage in a way that I thought made me sound knowledgeable and interesting. It didn't mean I didn't experience racism. I was told to 'go back to my own country' while walking down the street, had 'Black b*tch' shouted at me from a car, was called a n***** at school and 'horse mouth' on the bus by schoolboys referring to my big lips. I endured the company of a racist friend of a friend who was often invited to our house-share at university. He would freely relay what I now recognise as white supremacist views with very little challenge.

Often, when you are mixed race, people feel they have more freedom to express racist rhetoric in front of you because you won't be as 'offended'. I've heard the phrases: 'Yes, but you're not really Black', or: 'Your mum's white; you know what I mean' as justifications for their bile, as if I could just detach myself from my identity. There are also the 'colour-blind' comments such as 'I don't see colour' – as if ignoring the colour of our skin is a compliment and we should be happy (and remain silent) about the erasure of our Blackness.

I was lucky enough to spend time with both my parents' families growing up. My Jamaican family were based in Nottingham and it's only looking back that I appreciate the importance of having them all in my life. I have warm memories of my Aunt Gloria. She was the matriarch of the family and held us all together. When we went to visit her, as soon as the door opened, we were immediately hit with the smell of cooking. Jerk fish, fried plantain, callaloo, rice and peas. I would eat Jamaican food, have my hair done and spend time with my cousins. When I was with my Black family, I felt like I could finally relax. The expectations I had put on myself to perform were no longer there. However, I was aware that there were some differences, and my cousins and I weren't entirely the same. Our hair texture was different, as was our skin colour, we listened to different music, most of their friends were Black and I didn't really have any Black friends. These things led me to feel like I was a racial impostor at times. There was also the issue of where we grew up. Back then, our hometown of Margate was incredibly run-down. There were limited career opportunities and this, coupled with the government's drive at the time to see as many young people as possible getting into higher education, meant I left to go to university as soon as I finished my A-levels. It was only upon returning to visit in the holidays that I realised the depth of the socio-economic deprivation there was. Visiting friends in their hometowns of London, Bath and Guernsey, I became acutely aware that I was from a very working-class area that I'm sad to say felt like another source of shame.

One of the things I did talk about with pride was that artist Tracey Emin came from Margate. I had become a fan after my mum introduced me to her work. I distinctly remember starting to read about feminism and female empowerment off the back of seeing 'My Bed' and feeling hopeful that such exciting things could come out of our neglected seaside town.

One of the lesser-known things about Tracey Emin (she/her) is that she is of mixed-race heritage. Her mother was white and of Romanichal

heritage, her father was Turkish Cypriot, and her great-grandfather was a Sudanese enslaved man in the Ottoman Empire. We spoke to her about growing up in our hometown.

Naomi and Natalie: How would you identify, and has that changed at all?

Tracey: When I was young, I really felt half-Turkish. That's because when we were little, my dad was around a lot more and he had a lot of Turkish and Cypriot friends. Then, when we moved down to Margate, a lot of his friends were Greek Cypriots. Even though he was Turkish Cypriot, all his friends spoke Greek.

Naomi and Natalie: Would you say the cultural influence on you was there?

Tracey: Yes. I grew up eating Turkish food, listening to music and [I] experienced other cultures that were different. Margate was the Mediterranean on the English coast. But it wasn't like we promoted Turkish culture, because the Greek people in Margate had a much stronger identity and my dad spoke fluent Greek.

Naomi and Natalie: Growing up in Margate, did you see or experience racism?

Tracey: I was growing up in Margate [during] the seventies and it was different. First, my mum had a lot of racism thrown at her because she was with my dad. He was dark-skinned because my great-grandfather was from Sudan. [My great-grandfather] was a slave in the Ottoman Empire. My grandfather was Black. My dad grew up in Cyprus in a Greek village, so he spoke Turkish – but with a Greek accent – and English with a Greek accent, even though he was Turkish Cypriot.

When my mum was pregnant, she had a lot of abuse from people calling her a 'n****r lover'. When [my twin brother and I] were born, people would say things like, 'Oh, what lovely little mulatto babies.' When we were at school, quite often my dad was called a 'w**'. I remember going home and asking my mom what a 'w**' was, and she said, 'Western oriental gentleman', but this was in the early seventies and my dad was dark-skinned. Meanwhile, the war broke out in Cyprus between the Greeks and the Turks, and a number of our Greek friends stopped talking to us, which was very sad because the Mediterranean community in Margate was strong and vibrant. They owned the hotels, the cafes, the bars and the nightclubs. It was like a real community and a lot of my dad's friends were Greek and from Cyprus. So, growing up, I had a very strong Mediterranean identity.

Naomi and Natalie: You mentioned about your great-grandfather being a Sudanese enslaved man. Did learning that have any impact on you?

Tracey: My dad had told me about it when we were going to Cyprus on the boat. He told me, 'Your great-grandfather did the same journey. He was a slave in the Ottoman Empire; he was kidnapped on the banks of the Nile.' It all just sounded like an amazing story. But then, the reality of slavery and reality of how it is, is shocking. Also, in Cyprus, there were people called the 'Black Turks' and they were the slaves that were given their freedom in the island of Cyprus. My great-grandfather was one of them; he was given sheep and his freedom [in] around the 1890s.

Naomi and Natalie: Did you feel a sense of pride about your mixed heritage?

Tracey: Yeah, and I still do. Somehow with my position and presence as an artist in the 1990s, my Turkish heritage was never recognised. Other elements of my life were pushed to the forefront; however, my heritage was ignored. It was the same when I was a student in the 1980s – no one was remotely interested.

Naomi and Natalie: And we have to tell you, on a personal level, coming from Margate, often people would talk down about Margate, and we felt a bit embarrassed sometimes when we were younger. One thing that always gave us a sense of pride was that you were from here. It's important for you to know that you really did inspire so many people.

Tracey: Let me tell you something – that is really nice. I was so scared about moving back to Margate because I thought maybe people might be a bit off with me or something. But it's brilliant and, especially in the town, people shake your hand [and say] 'Just wanted to tell you, thanks a lot; if it wasn't for you, I wouldn't have this job or this work.' It's such a nice, positive thing compared to how it was twenty years ago. People have really changed and it's much more optimistic, and you can see how the town is improving. So, no need to feel ashamed; you can hold your head up with pride.

For us, growing up in a white-majority town is our coming-of-age story. For Alexis* (she/her), this wasn't always the case. She spoke to us about her experience of moving from east London to Brighton and being the only queer woman of colour in her community group.

Alexis: I am in my late twenties and I identify as a queer woman of colour. My dad is from Barbados, so I'm half-Bajan and half-British. I grew up in south-east London with my mum, my dad, my older sister,

---

*Some names appear with an asterisk and have been changed to protect the privacy of interviewees who wanted to remain anonymous.

my older brother (for a short period of time) and my younger brother. My older brother was adopted, and he is of mixed heritage that is different to mine.

Natalie and Naomi: How was your experience of growing up as a mixed-race person?

Alexis: My experience of being mixed in south London was a funny one, because I don't think I ever realised it, except for a few key moments at school. South-east London has a huge Caribbean community and there weren't many white people where I grew up. It was very mixed. It was Caribbean people and lots of people from South Asian backgrounds. I never noticed until a few occasions at secondary school. I went to a local state school that was a bit rough and there were only two mixed-race girls, but actually what people meant by that was there were only two *white and Black* mixed-race girls. There were other mixed-race people, but they were not referred to as mixed because they were not white and Black. There was a moment at school where one of the English teachers said to me, 'You had a tough upbringing; you had it rough growing up.' I was so confused, and then they said, 'You don't really know your dad, do you?'

I said, 'Yes I do – I live with my dad!' She'd just made this story up about my life in her head. It was so weird, and back then I thought, *She's crazy.* It wasn't until I got home that I realised what [had] happened and why she thought that. The biggest shock was going to university in Brighton. I think growing up in London there's so much culture and people are really proud; you go to the corner shop and there is every spice under the sun. You go down the road, there's the Black hair shop, but in Brighton there was none of that. I'd have to come back to London to get my hair done and things like that. I knew I was different there.

Natalie and Naomi: When you moved to Brighton, did you know anything about it? Did you think it would be more multicultural?

Alexis: People love to have these statements about Brighton being 'so diverse'. Really, what they mean is there's a lot of gay white men in Brighton, and that's kind of where it ends. I knew there was a huge gay community. When I was going to uni, I knew that I wasn't straight, but I wasn't going to Brighton because it was a queer-affirming place; it was my second choice of university. Maybe I assumed that there would be more Black families – I knew there wouldn't be as many as London or a bigger city like Birmingham or Manchester. Then I think I was just shocked because it felt almost squashed down. Security guards were Black; cleaners were Black. I would always say hello, but it felt as though I [had] walked into a time warp. Even on the bus, people would clutch onto their purses when I got on. My friends who were Black and queer left Brighton pretty quickly after we graduated. I stayed and worked, and I think one of the things I've been reflecting on is they probably did it right. When the murder of George Floyd happened, I got a message from every person under the sun in Brighton, from people I didn't even talk to. I realised, *Oh, I am the only dark person you know*. At that point, I said to my parents, 'When my tenancy runs out, I'm coming back to London, because I can't do this.'

Natalie and Naomi: What was your experience being a queer Person of Colour living in a white-majority town?

Alexis: I think being a Person of Colour in the queer community in Brighton is tough, and I couldn't even imagine what it was like to be a trans Person of Colour in the queer community. When my Black queer friends left Brighton, I didn't feel safe in the community anymore. It's still a really big problem, I would say, there's a lot of fetishisation of the Black body in the queer community, and that's something I didn't realise. I guess I had the assumption that we won't be oppressed because the gay community is already oppressed, and they know what it's like for someone to call you names or spit on you in the street or they know what it's like to be frightened every time you walk down a street. But maybe they don't see it the same or they choose not to see what they're doing. So when some people in the community left Brighton for their own mental health, which I didn't even consider for myself, I was left thinking, *I'm Black and queer and a woman and alone.* I probably haven't realised it until now, how important the group of queer People of Colour at my uni was for me. I think the experience of being able to be myself with them allowed me to finally accept myself because it's people that look like you, who talk like you, behave like you, who have been through similar experiences as you. All of us seem to have this shared, familiar experience. It was so inspiring and empowering. I would think, *If you can do it, then so can I.*

Michael Crutchley (he/him) is from Kent. He was adopted at birth and raised by two white parents in a majority-white town alongside two mixed-race siblings. He is in his early forties and identifies as Black British. He spoke to us about some of his reflections on his upbringing.

Naomi: I know that you grew up in the same hometown as Natalie and me. What was it like for you growing up in a white-majority area?

Michael: I felt that I knew who I was, partly because it was made very obvious to me that I was different. I felt that I had some good friends that looked out for me. I think my upbringing could've been a lot worse had I not, maybe been a bit wiser to the situation. I have a brother who is ten years older than me, one of the first waves of Black people in the area, and he knew exactly what it was like. He grew up in the eighties and I grew up in the nineties. My parents were very generous and invested in us to attend a private school, which was very multicultural.

My parents knew that was something that would be important to my sister and I growing up but, in a sense, perhaps they sheltered us from some of that as well. In terms of those experiences, when I went out into the 'real world', when I left private school and went to grammar school and did extracurricular activities – football rather than dancing – I really felt it. So there was some more negative stuff that opened my eyes in the mid-nineties.

Naomi and Natalie: So, having the experience of being in a fairly international school almost felt like you were a bit sheltered? Was the school very multicultural, in comparison to the rest of the town?

Michael: Yes. If you looked at the class set there's fifteen in the class, eight or nine from Nigeria, [the] Maldives and the Middle East and then there was the odd local from down the road. It was really very diverse and that was kind of my outlook on life until the early to mid-nineties. Our family dynamics changed; my parents split up and we didn't have the money [we'd had before], so we moved schools. I remember my first week at my new school. One of the prefects stopped us in our tracks as we were scuttling around between classes, as you do in Year 7 or 8 and said to me, 'You're a bit dirty, aren't you?' My friends said, 'I can't believe this; we need to talk to someone.' The prefect said, 'Who are you going to tell?' and that's when I realised this isn't as much of a safe environment as my other school.

Growing up in a white-majority town was certainly challenging. There is no doubt that being Black or a Person of Colour in a space where you are the minority has a profound impact on your experience and how you form narratives around your identity. While our hometown is more diverse than it ever has been, there are other complexities, such as gentrification and class segregation. Liberal sentiments do not necessarily equate to anti-racism. In fact, there is a whole lot of white exceptionalism that occurs here. It has taken time, therapy and finding others with common experiences to help us to heal. Some of what we have written may resonate with you, and if that's the case, we hope you also find the space to process your experiences and heal too.

Chapter 2

'What are you?':

On race

~~

Naomi and Natalie: One of our greatest fears about writing a book was that once your words are in print, you are unable to edit or revise them. There are things that we wrote a matter of months ago that we would choose to rephrase or challenge now. Our thoughts and ideas about race have changed and developed as we have learned more from others and about ourselves. We accept that there are things that we will do and say now that we will reconsider and change our minds about in the future and there's nothing apocryphal about that. In fact, questioning why we believe what we believe is healthy.

A life lived in an echo chamber without a willingness to listen to others and be challenged on why we actually believe what we believe is not revolutionary or progressive. Without a doubt, the most challenging work we have done this past year is to reconsider what we both thought we knew about race and how we identify. This is not us telling you what you should call yourself, but an insight into the journey of discomfort and dismantling what we thought we understood about race. Most notably, it involves coming to the realisation that consistently talking about race as a binary, as if it were based on a biological fact, has contributed to upholding the system of racism rather than attempting to destroy it.

~~~

Naomi: When I was younger, I was mesmerised by the sight of multiracial families, particularly those who had children. Margate in the 1980s was not diverse. If I saw a mixed-race couple or family on the street, I would smile inside. Firstly, because I recognised family structures similar to mine, but also because I romanticised them and somehow thought it was representative of the end of racism. Basking in my childhood innocence, my thought process was, if people from different races could be in a relationship together and even have children together, that would mean prejudice would decrease. They might even have an impact on their wider friends and family. I was caught up in the idea of some kind of mixed-race utopia. When I first met my husband (who is white), I would nudge him every time I saw a couple who looked like us, as if to signal to him that we were part of something progressive and important. I now know that this is not the reality I thought it was, and that it's a problematic way of thinking.

The mixed-race population

Mixed-race people are often framed as something 'new' but, of course, they have been around for centuries. There is no doubt though that the mixed-race population is growing. In the 2021 book, *Biracial Britain*, author Remi Adekoya informs us that by the end of this century, the mixed-race population in the UK is set to rise to 30 per cent and by the end of 2150 it will grow to 75 per cent.[1] With the results of the 2021 census pending at the time of writing, the most recent figures published are from the 2011 census, where it was recorded that there were over 1,2 million mixed-race Britons (2.3 per cent of the population).[2] The number of mixed-race children under four rose from 116,000 in 2001, to 220,000 in 2011, with the BBC documentary, *Mixed Britannia* noting that one in ten British children are growing up in interracial households. Despite this, growing up, there was quite literally nothing we could read or access to help us understand ourselves better. There was a distinct lack of conversation about the mixed-race identity and when there was, the focus was heavily centred around '"Black" and "white"' people.

Journalist Matthew Ryder, who wrote an article for the *Guardian* titled 'What does Archie tell us about mixed-race Britain?' stated the following:

First, interracial relationships and the growing mixed-race population is something the British Black community is experiencing in
exceptionally higher numbers compared with other groups. According to the 2011 census, members of the Black community are
among the most likely to choose a white partner – close to 50 per
cent for Black Caribbeans. (In contrast, those with heritage from
the Indian subcontinent generally have a rate of interracial relationships that is much lower.) This likelihood also increases with each
new generation: the chances of people of mixed Black/white
heritage having a white partner, are about 80 per cent. The
demographic implications of this for the future of Black Caribbeans
in Britain are obvious.[3]

There are, of course, many different factors that impact this.

Around the world

The 2000 census was the first in the history of the United States to offer the population the option of identifying themselves as belonging to more than one race. Before this, Dr Chinelo L. Njaka told us, 'the term "mixed race" appeared on past US censuses as "mulatto", "quadroon" and "octoroon" well before self-enumeration began in 1970.'

In 2010, 2.9 per cent of the US population identified as 'two or more races', which equates to almost 10 million people. In 2020 this surged to 10.2 per cent, which equates to 33.8 million people with nearly half of all multiracial Americans being under eighteen years old.[4] Pew Research's 'Multiracial in America' report projects that the multiracial population will triple by 2060.[5] The growth of mixed-race people as a demographic isn't exclusive to the UK and the US. In the Dominican Republic and Cuba, mixed-race people officially make up the majority of the population and according to the 2016 South African census, the mixed-race population is the second largest ethnic group at 8.8 per cent, behind Black Africans at 80.8 per cent. Many people have interpreted the growth in numbers of multiracial people as a symbol of progression, but, as we know, there are many complexities to growing up within a multiracial family and to attribute anti-racist progression to the rise of mixed-race people is problematic.

I have never seen so many conversations take place in the mainstream about race. There are an abundance of books that grapple with the subjects of colonialism, imperialism and enslavement, as well as anti-racism, identity and race. Yet many of our conversations and writing still seem to underpin the myth that race is a biological fact rather than a social construct. Before we continue, we must address the importance of our understanding about race in the first place.

More and more, we are aware that we have been taught through a lens of 'whiteness'. The history we thought we knew was skewed to uphold a particular narrative. The people we were told to respect and idolise were never advocating for us. There was a myriad of things about our history that we were never taught in school, never asked to examine, never discussed with our parents or friends, never researched or began to discover until now. And above all, the simple fact remains that nobody told us 'race' was created entirely for one group of people to create capital and retain power over another.

So, what is the big obsession with race?

To attempt to understand ourselves, we need to know where we come from. It doesn't mean it has to define us, but it can certainly help us shape and prepare for a better future. We've all heard the phrase, 'There's only one race: the human race', but what does that actually mean? Where do we get our understanding about racial identity in the first place?

In the two-part BBC documentary, *Britain's Forgotten Slave Owners*, historian David Olusoga explores the abolition of slavery, which included alarming information about the government's compensation package to enslavers. The first episode starts in Barbados where, in 1627, a group of approximately fifty British settlers arrived on the island and it was there that the first slave society was created using enslaved African people. Olusoga then goes on to speak to Professor Sir Hilary Beckles from the University of the West Indies who explains:

> All the societies in the hemisphere had enslaved peoples, but Barbados was the first to be built and sustained completely upon the enslavement of Africans, with no alternative system of economic development.[6]

It was there that the 1661 Barbados Slave Code was invented, which was based on English common law that dealt with convicts and servants who absconded from their duties. At this time, the only way to ensure there was no uprising from the workers (including both enslaved people and labourers) was to create a hierarchy based on skin colour. Thus, the construct that is 'whiteness' was created as a means of control, synonymous with power and, along with 'scientific racism', used as justification for supremacy. These slaves codes were a means of enforcing racialised violence and a way to legally torture, abuse and murder human beings based on skin colour.[7]

By the eighteenth century race was being treated as biological fact and in the 1776 edition of his book, *On the Natural Variety of Mankind*, German scientist Johann Friedrich Blumenbach is believed to have created one of the first race-based classifications. He decided on five categories: 'Caucasian, the white race; Mongolian, the yellow race; Malayan, the brown race; Ethiopian, the black race, and American, the red race.'[8]

Jenée Desmond-Harris, in her *Vox* article, '11 ways race isn't real', writes:

> If 'whites' were in their own category – with innate differences backed by science – then that category could be deemed superior.

45

As a result, they could justify their own rights and freedoms while enslaving, excluding, and otherwise mistreating people who had been placed in different racial categories.

So the division of people into groups based on general geographical origins of their ancestors or descriptions of the way they look, is the basis of a manmade strategy for making sense of treating some people better than others.[9]

While race can be defined as 'a category of humankind that shares certain distinctive physical traits',[10] there is no genetic test that can be used to determine or verify race. As science journalist and author Angela Saini said, 'Race science is not about biology, it's about power. It's a game we've been playing for hundreds of years, and we're still playing it today.'[11] As human beings, we share over 99 per cent of our genetic material with one another but racial classifications were used to justify white supremacy and these continue to impact power, wealth and opportunities, which uniquely shape how we experience the world.

~~~

Natalie: Sometimes people will call me Black but, on the whole, I call myself mixed race. Understanding that race is a construct and was created with the intention of creating division means I have now become more comfortable with referring to my heritage instead, by referring to myself as Jamaican and English. I know I am, on the whole, racialised as Black and have absolutely no problem with being referred to as such. I'm proud to be aligned with my community, but the notion that I strictly belong to one or even two racial categories, and therefore have some sort of fixed parameters in which I can connect with the world, reinforces the very thing that we are trying to fight against.

~~

'What are you?'
'Is that really your mum?'
'Is that really your dad?'
'You don't look . . .'
'I love mixed-race babies!'
'Oh, you're half-caste.'
'That's so exotic!'
'Are you sure you haven't got any . . . in you?'
'Where are you *really* from?'
'Are you adopted?'

How many of these sound familiar?

Racial microaggressions

Racial microaggressions are defined as subtle statements or incidents that mask underlying prejudice by being presented in a way that may be perceived as harmless, such as a joke or a compliment.[12] For example, 'Your English is really good!' or, 'You're very good-looking, for a Black person.'

The implied meanings in statements like this not only makes it particularly difficult to articulate or identify why hearing them feels uncomfortable, but they can also be accompanied by gaslighting (the term 'gaslighting' stems from the 1938 play *Gas Light* then 1940 film, *Gaslight*, which depicted a husband who, by slowly turning down the gas-fuelled lamps in their home and insisting his wife is imagining it, attempts to cause her to question her own sanity).[13] Examples of gaslighting include phrases like: 'It was only a joke!' or: 'Don't be so sensitive', after hurtful comments have been made. These were the most common phrases we found in our interviews, which relate directly to the mixed-race experience.

In the USA there are thousands of people who identify as Afro-Indigenous or Black-Indigenous. The histories of Black and Indigenous people are inextricably linked, but our fixed ideas about what certain groups should look like can lead to others feeling like outsiders. Afro-Indigenous model and writer Kara Roselle Smith, who is Chappaquiddick Wampanoag of the Wampanoag Nation, uses her platform to speak about the lack of Afro-Indigenous representation within the media and beauty industries. In an interview with *Coveteur*, she says: 'I'm Afro-Indigenous and I present very Black. Oftentimes, I would voice that I was also Native American and children at school would be like, "No you're not" or "Are you sure?"'[14]

Common misconceptions about being mixed race:

1. You have a white parent.
2. You are light-skinned.
3. You identify as 'mixed race'. (It is everyone's personal decision as to how they choose to identify.)
4. You have to choose a side of your mixed-race identity to align with.
5. You are a homogenous group. (There may be commonalities in experience, but many things such as class, gender, ethnicity and geographical location will impact this.)
6. You are confused or lost.

For more on microaggressions, see Chapter 4 (pp. 80–103).

~~~~~

Chinelo L. Njaka, PhD (she/her) is in her early forties and is the co-author of the book, *Mixed Race in the US and UK: Comparing the Past, Present and Future*. She identifies as mixed race.

Naomi and Natalie: You're an academic; please tell us about your background and what led you to your academic studies?

Chinelo: My dad was Igbo from Nigeria, and he was an immigrant to the US. My mum is Black American, which really means that she has a Black mother and father who was half-white, quarter Native American and quarter Black. So that's where my mixture comes in. In the US, and especially growing up in the South, that meant she was Black. The US is really colour-coded and even my parents raised me that way; they raised me as a Black American but that never worked for me and my experience. My Nigerian father was an influence on my life and gave me a different experience than other people that had two Black American parents. I grew up in a Jewish neighbourhood and then went to schools where I was the only Black kid in my grade.

When I switched schools, there was another mixed-race person there and it was amazing that there were two of us. As I grew up there were more Black kids. In my graduating class, when I finished school there were about ten of us among five hundred children. I was always sticking out as the only Black person in my class but even with that, when there were other Black students, I never fit in. Thinking about that now, I think it's because I wasn't socialised completely as a Black American. I had that Nigerian influence. I suppose it's the common story of not fitting in; I didn't fit in there and it was the same on the Nigerian side because I had this American mother. I never fit in with white people. I always felt as though there was a separation or that it was a token thing.

Fast-forward to my Master's programme where I started [exploring identity and race]. We were having to write about identity, and I started talking about being mixed race and the lecturer said, 'This is really interesting; you should do a PhD.' I finished my Master's programme here in the UK, went back home to the US and really started sitting with it. Being at home and feeling even more displaced and thinking about this identity stuff, I thought, maybe I could do something more. I started doing work around Blackness and how ethnicity fits into ideas of Blackness and trying to stretch this idea of Blackness a bit in a way that was more inclusive. At the time there was this idea of what Black was and what Black wasn't, and I just knew I wasn't it, but I felt very Black, and I was growing in my love and appreciation of Blackness. Then I came to the UK. I remember filling out a form about my race for the first time, being so confused by the long list because it wasn't just the colours [that you have in the US], and I didn't know what I was supposed to select because it was, Black African, Black Caribbean and Black Other. I was part African, but part American, so I had no idea what to select. So when I started my PhD, I started reading about being mixed race because I saw very close overlaps between my personal experiences and the questions I had and what I was reading in mixed-race literature. Then it became this way to examine and be critical about the notions of race, how race was made and how race changes across time and space. How much this one social construct taken alone, or intersectionally organises people's lives. While I was studying it, I found there was a community around the few people that were studying it. It just felt like that was where I needed to be.

Naomi and Natalie: What would you say are some of the issues with the term 'mixed race' or 'biracial'?

Chinelo: 'Mixed race' seems to be the catch-all term. The Critical Mixed Race Study Association uses the term 'mixed race'. It definitely has some issues. I think just talking about race generally, it relies on essential notions of race – this idea that race is a concrete thing; it's fixed; it has certain meanings that don't change over time and space. I guess there's no real good term and there's no term that would be good for everybody. It's a confusing one. It's not perfect, but it is the one that we use, and I don't know why we use it, but it's the one that people come under and then have the space to critique it and say why it's not perfect. Another issue with it is that it's an amalgamation of immense diversity.

'Mixed race' doesn't really mean anything, because it can encompass so many different things, and you can't really meaningfully group people together under a term. So if you have 'mixed race' as a general term, it doesn't have the nuance to talk about specific people's experiences. Everyone under that label has their own unique experience and there might be some similarities between and among people, but the specificities are lost. It's considered as a race and race isn't fixed; it's different depending on where you are and so, what's considered a race in some places, might just be the colour of your skin, or phenotypic things, and in another place it could be more about what area of a country you're from or what religion you are.

There are all sorts of different things of what can be considered a 'race'. So, when you put all that together again, it can be very broad and almost everyone could be considered mixed race if you really wanted to stretch it. I ask myself, 'How long until "race" is deluded?' I think what I mean by this is: when does mixing so-called races become no longer mixed? Another thought I had is that culture, ethnicity and other forms of heritage that fit in the mixed-race experience depend on where you are. Those things actually determine what race you are locally, but then if you move to a different place, it may not matter so much. I suppose it's fraught with all these inconsistencies that people don't really think about. When you talk about the concept of race, wherever you happen to be, people usually have very clear ideas of what this is, and who belongs to what group, but when you really start talking about it, it ceases to make sense.

Within the US context, biracial, I think, almost certainly means Black and white. You can be from different racialised groups and not be Black or white, and so there's a problem that I see with this. I guess it's better than mixed race, because it's not talking about mixing or mixing in a pot. I haven't heard people talking about themselves as multiracial. 'Multiracial' seems like more of an academic or an official sort of term, which is fine. Race is such a weird thing that I have more questions than I do answers. That's why it's fascinating to me, because there are just so many questions.

Chinelo: Can I ask you both a question? In terms of grappling with your identity, I'm assuming that you have thought through the question of, 'Can you be considered Black?' Can you be considered mixed race? Has the question of, 'Can you be considered white?' ever even really entered your minds, or has that been a possibility?

Natalie: For me personally, no. Unless I passed as white, I wouldn't ever consider myself as white. I understand I am light-skinned, but I have never been mistaken for a white person.

Naomi: I think the added part to that is that we have grown up in a very white-majority area. So it might be different if we lived in parts of London or [other] multicultural areas but, for us, there was no one else, so we were 'the Black people' in our town. And I think that has made a real difference to how we perceived ourselves growing up. We were always used as 'the Black person', whether it was in our school, friendship groups, etc.

Chinelo: Yes, that was my experience as well. I do have white heritage, but it would never be even acknowledged as such. So whiteness was never an ethnicity or an identity that I was ever going to have. I can relate to being 'the Black friend' or 'the token friend'.

Naomi and Natalie: A lot of conversation around race in the mainstream, particularly in the last year or so, has focused on binaries such as Black and white. Why do you think it's important for people to understand that race is actually a social construct?

Chinelo: I think it's important to understand what race is and what function it serves. I'm reading and working on research that tries to push this idea that race is a social construct, and race as a social construct needs to be pushed a bit further to understand what it means. Something I've noticed is, it seems as if more and more people know that race is a social construct but when they start talking about it, they usually fall into biological understandings of race, where they describe what it is or try to determine what race a person is. Or they'll start talking in stereotypes about how Black people are always good athletes or something, and it's really weird.

So, racism is a social construction of what? I'm a social scientist and I think even social scientists can't really explain what that actually means. There are now researchers putting forward this idea that race is constructed for the purposes of upholding white supremacy and used as a tool to separate people and maintain political power. When I read that, I thought, *That's powerful.* It opens up new ideas for why race and racism is persistent, despite the now more-mainstream idea that race is a social construct (the Black and white binary could be an example of this power play). So, society has been structured along this faux binary where whiteness is good, at best, desired, and Blackness is bad, worse, undesirable. Then, as more diversity has come into our societies, they get organised along this binary. I am embarrassed to say that I didn't notice this right away, but the UK census seems to be organised by colour, it starts with white, ends with Black; it's white, mixed race, Asian, Caribbean, African. It's a colour hierarchy of some sort. So we need to be asking ourselves, Who decided on this? Who benefits from this paradigm? Why has it lasted despite more modern ideas of race and racism? And even though we move towards mainstreaming anti-racism, why is it still here? It's actually about looking at it more radically, if that's the right word. It's created by white supremacy to uphold white supremacy.

Naomi and Natalie: We sometimes just wonder if we've fallen into the ultimate trap. If we think about enslavement and racial categorisation, the basis of both is rooted in ensuring white people maintain power. To eradicate racism, all of us coming together is the most powerful thing we could do; therefore, it works well for this system to keep us all in separate categories.

Chinelo: This whole thing about 'BAME' [Black, Asian, Minority, Ethnic] – it's such a complex thing. I don't like the term, but when the conversations are around what people prefer, they say their ethnicity or heritage. But, if you split people up like that, is that the same division that white supremacy is trying to do in the first place? It just seems to be some sort of house of mirrors, no matter which way you go. As Audre Lorde said, 'The master's tools will never dismantle the master's house.' Living under it and growing up under it and having it last for centuries, how do you even imagine a society that isn't under white supremacy?

Anna Masing (she/her) is in her early forties. She is a writer, poet and academic. She explores with us her thoughts about the term 'mixed race'.

Naomi and Natalie: How do you identify?

Anna: South East Asian (SEA) in general, as I am read as 'not white'. I identify with being Asian and try to specify my SEA heritage. I usually say that I am mixed race – white and SEA Indigenous. The Indigenous identity is very specific within the SEA identity and I am trying to be more explicit about that. My dad is Iban, an Indigenous community in Borneo, and my mother is a white New Zealander (mainly of Scottish heritage).

Naomi and Natalie: What do you think of the term 'mixed race'?

Anna: I like this term, as it encompasses the idea of mixed culture too. I feel very much both Western/Global North, as well as having very clear anchors in being SEA and what that means. I also feel it is very important to recognise the ambiguity of being mixed race – that privilege of being able to move through various spaces, of being unidentifiable.

Naomi and Natalie: Have you ever experienced any racism? Would you mind sharing an example of how that has shown up in your life?

Anna: This links with the idea of being mixed race, because I am hard to place into a specific 'box', or people can't work out what 'non-white' I am. The racism I get is not as direct and violent, mostly. I mainly get sexualised racism . . . the intersection of exotic and erotic is where I feel I sit, which is a different kind of violence. This manifests from strangers on the street saying things, to the way men flirt with me.

The first time I remember being racialised is at primary school, when a boy in New Zealand spat out words about being Samoan. I knew it was hateful and I responded with, 'But I'm not Samoan,' thinking why on earth he'd said it in a hateful way, as well as what was wrong with being Samoan. It was how I realised that not being white was an 'issue'. It was the only thing he could think of, in his need to be mean.

I also remember overhearing a woman say to my mother that brown girls develop quicker than white girls – she meant sexually – I would've been about eight. I think this was the first time I had realised the danger of being different.

~~~

Honest conversations about the construction of race and stark implications that racial identities have on our life are crucial. Some of the confusion around our own identity emanated from not understanding why race was constructed or how systemic racism manifests in everyday life. It's important that we continue to expand our knowledge and understanding of this in order to subvert the current trap we fall into, which is to place so much emphasis on race as a fixed identity. It's no wonder some of us have been left feeling like we don't belong.

Chapter 3

'No, but where are you *really* from?':

On identity

~~

'Where are you from?'

'Margate.'

'But where are you *really* from?'

'I was born in Margate, then I moved to London and then came back.'

'Yes, but I mean where is *this* from?' *gestures to my face*

'Oh, you mean, why am I not white?'

Naomi: To be mixed race can often mean navigating different worlds and, at times, feeling as though you are not fully a part of either. There are moments when you feel caught in the middle; that you need to choose a side or feel distant from parts of your heritage. Being asked variations of the question, 'What are you?' can ultimately leave you wondering where you fit and questioning who you are. Growing up in England in the 1980s, the terms I was most commonly referred to as were the offensive words 'half-caste' or 'coloured', while Mum and Dad would call me 'mixed race'. There was little understanding about most things to do with racial identity where we were. The term 'half-caste' comes from the Latin word, 'castus', meaning pure, and the Spanish and Portuguese derivative 'casta', which means race.[1] Essentially, the term signifies that if you are mixed race, you are half 'pure'. Another term that was used was 'half-breed', which the Collins English Dictionary defines as 'a person whose parents are of different races',[2] referring particularly to the offspring of a white person and Native American. Obviously, both terms are equally derogatory. Even now, you might hear the terms being thrown around, but the legacy of the meaning lingers. It says, 'You are half of something and not fully whole.'

Sarah from Mixed Bloom shares her thoughts on identity:

Naomi and Natalie: What are some of the things that you might say to people who are of mixed heritage and who may be struggling to understand where they fit in the world?

Sarah: I would have to say that the first thing I think is the most important is to understand and truly know that 'mixed' is a thing. That's the baseline. We don't get that being mixed is the baseline. It is a whole thing. And there's no need to go look for affirmation outside. We look for affirmation within mixedness, with other mixed people. Looking for affirmation from monoracial people doesn't make any sense. Mixed is a whole thing, but we have been denied that as just a basic reality. It's non-negotiable. We shouldn't be negotiating about these things.

There are so many variables to identity and mixed is certainly *an* identity. When we talk about all the different mixes and all these bottom-line similarities, that's just another indication that it is something, because you have people from all different mixes who have all these similarities in their experiences – because of looking for information from monoracial people.

Natalie: All our experiences differ, but after speaking to over twenty people from a range of different backgrounds about growing up mixed race, there are definite commonalities: one of which is the feeling of being considered 'not enough' of anything to fully claim either identity. As a child, I was acutely aware from a young age that I wasn't white. My skin was never light enough to be considered as such. My hair wouldn't lie flat and was described by the dinner ladies at my infant school as 'candy floss' – another indicator that made me feel as though

I was different to the other children. However, at the same time, I wasn't Black like my dad or dark enough to feel I could consider myself as such. Wrestling with these issues can leave you feeling confused about your identity, particularly when no one is having these conversations around you. I am more hopeful for younger people in this respect. There has never been more open discussion about race and access to writing on being mixed race. In the process of writing this book, the majority of people we interviewed (of our generation or older) noted that it took them years of exploration to finally be at ease with how they identify and understand themselves. I'm no exception to this, hence why I hope that this book brings about change for future generations. I hope that they will not have the same difficult experiences we did or have to resort to the same survival tactics that I and others have relied on to help us move through life, such as altering our appearance, suppressing parts of ourselves, or code-switching.

Code-Switching

The *Merriam-Webster Dictionary* describes code-switching as: 'switching from the linguistic system of one language or dialect to that of another.'[3]

Many Black, Indigenous and People of Colour (BIPOC) will be familiar with the practice of code-switching and behaving differently, depending on the space you are in. It's the way we communicate in specific social groups and situations. This can range from accents and dialects to tone of voice and the language we use/adopt in these circumstances. A prime example of this is seen in the 2018 film, *Sorry to Bother You*, in which actor LaKeith Stanfield plays Black call-centre worker Cassius Green, who discovers that if he uses his 'white voice' he will sell more products for the company.[4]

We all code-switch across social contexts, no matter our race, but when it comes to being mixed race, it can sometimes feel as though we are code-switching all the time. For some of you reading this book, you may not feel this way at all, but for others, you may feel as though you need to act one way for one side of your family and another way for the other.

Racial impostor syndrome

Racial impostor syndrome refers to a feeling of discord when it comes to your racial heritage[5] and another way in which mixed-race people question their identity. It's a feeling of self-doubt, in which you can feel like you don't fully belong, and where other people's perceptions of your racial identity don't match how you identify. It also means you can feel as if you have to prove yourself. It's the sense that you're not enough. It also manifests in people reminding you that you're only 'half of this or a quarter of that'. It can impact your behaviour and make you feel anxious. We remember going to Jamaica and being worried about ordering Jamaican food in case we pronounced it wrong – do we say plan-tin or plan-tayne? Racial impostor syndrome is not exclusive to multiracial people, but it goes without saying that this can be a very damaging experience. Not feeling as if they were 'enough' was a common theme from those we interviewed, and many found themselves compelled to validate their 'ethnic credentials'.

> 'Well, I am half-Jamaican.'
> 'I can cook jollof rice.'
> 'I can speak Hindi.'
> 'I lived with my Sri Lankan family for six months.'

Feeling 'inauthentic', or as if you are not 'enough' of anything, can make you self-conscious and destroy your self-esteem. I know mixed-race people who have tried various ways to gain acceptance from the racial groups they identify with, whether that is through their clothing, the food they eat, the language they study or books they read – only to be rejected or accused of inauthenticity. This can be a very lonely experience and again, problematic because it means that there are internalised beliefs of what each race exemplifies.

Natalie: When the Black Lives Matter movement began in 2013, I didn't know if it included me or not, and I began interrogating my identity. It wasn't until I started to read more about race and identity that I realised there were very few resources for mixed-race people. Reading forums, articles, social media posts and comments left me feeling disoriented. Some people quite clearly considered mixed-race people (those with one Black parent) to be Black and saw no issue with them identifying as such. However, I also read some commentary that suggested you had no right to claim you were Black if you had one non-Black parent, or that you shouldn't be speaking on behalf of Black people if you're mixed race. Our experience will no doubt have differences to that of a monoracial Black person but to be excluded from the narrative completely is erasure of identity. Shortly after starting our Instagram account, we shared a post about being mixed race, at which point someone decided to climb into our DMs.

> DM: Y'all love white folk, which is why your posts are this way.
>
> US: Can you explain what you mean?
>
> DM: With Caucasian blood coursing through your veins, you have no idea what true racism is, as you share DNA with the oppressor. It's like the police being part of its own investigation. Conflict of interest. Mixed folk can't speak for originals. You can only speak for your race.

It was at this point I realised how ludicrous it was trying to find affirmation about my identity through other people. Whilst the sentiment seemed to be: 'You're only Black if you're "100 per cent" Black', let's not forget that we live in a racialised society which will assign us into racial categories purely based on the way we look. Also, not all mixed-race people are automatically light-skinned and there will be those who are darker skinned than monoracial Black people. It made me consider that perhaps I'm not as confused as I thought – perhaps, I'm trying to find my way in a world that doesn't know where to place me.

'What are you?'

The question, 'What are you?' is common for mixed-race people. Usually prompted by strangers or those you have just met, whether on a date, at a job interview, a drink at the pub or meeting your friends' parents for the first time. No matter how many times I have been asked this question, I am still somewhat taken aback when I hear it. It's loaded, it's intrusive and it is often directed to mixed-race people because we are not seen as fitting into the binaries of racial categorisation. While some direct this question from a place of genuine interest in our heritage or background, for others, it carries an interrogatory tone – as if they are trying to find out how and why we belong here.

Some people don't want to talk about their heritage with strangers or those they have just met. For some it may be a trigger to something, perhaps a difficult relationship, upbringing or a trauma. While I'm happy to talk about my Jamaican and English heritage, I'm not interested in questions which are essentially rooted in asking me to justify and explain why I am not racialised as white, and this presentiment of being 'othered' will be familiar to many of you reading this.

Unless you're white passing, you will often face being racialised as anything other than white because of the way racial categories were established. 'Whiteness' is set up in a way that it does not simply allow you to choose. Whiteness is predicated upon white 'purity'. History shows us that mixed-race people were never allowed to just 'choose a side', especially not their white side. Social and legal principles of racial classification such as the 'one-drop rule', which originated in the US during the twentieth century, demonstrate this. Also known as the 'one Black ancestor rule', it meant that a single drop of 'Black blood' was enough to racially categorise a person as Black, therefore mixed-race people could not/cannot be categorised as white.

In 1977, Susie Guillory Phipps (a woman who considered herself white) was applying for her passport and requested a copy of her birth certificate. When she received the document, she was shocked to discover that the state of Louisiana classified her as 'colored' due to the fact that she had 3/32 parts 'Negro blood'. Tracing her ancestry, Phipps discovered that her great-great-great-great-grandmother was a Black enslaved woman by the name of Margarita, and in the state of Louisiana, if you had at least 3 per cent Black ancestry you were classified as such. A lawsuit ensued and Phipps spent $20,000 on legal fees to force Louisiana to change her birth certificate. In 1983, Louisiana repealed the law.[6]

Racial 'passing'

Racial passing, according to the *Cambridge Dictionary*, 'is a situation in which a person who belongs to a particular group is believed by other people to be a member of a different group'.[7] The term is commonly applied to BIPOC who have a lighter skin tone or hair texture, which enables them to 'pass' for white. In some cases, this can be utilised to gain certain benefits and privileges. Historically, the ability to 'pass' for white was used in order to escape enslavement and laws of racial discrimination.

In the article 'What it means to be white passing if you're BIPOC', Taylyn Washington-Harmon states:

> White passing isn't new; enslaved African-Americans would attempt to pass as white to escape enslavement or subjugation. Even after slavery was outlawed, lighter-skinned people of colour would try to pass for white for political and social gain, and also as a survival tactic.[8]

However, we both find the term 'white passing' extremely problematic. First, it centres whiteness again, making it the default by which everyone is measured. Second, it implies that a person is purposefully disassociating themselves from their heritage; it essentially acts as a way to erase part of someone's identity.

In June 2020 musician Halsey, who is biracial, announced that she is white passing, in response to a tweet criticising her for not 'claiming her Black side' when she posted in the wake of the murder of George Floyd.

> *I'm white passing. It's not my place to say 'we'. It's my place to help. I am in pain for my family, but nobody is going to kill me based on my skin colour. I've always been proud of who I am, but it'd be an absolute disservice to say 'we' when I'm not susceptible to the same violence.*[9]

In this case (and the same can be said for the experiences that some light-skinned people may face) it's important to address the advantages that come with being in closer proximity to whiteness than monoracial Black people. It's also vital to acknowledge how interpersonal racism can play out in other ways, for example, people finding out one or both of your parents are not white and treating you differently, or having a sibling with a different skin complexion to you and people not believing you are related, or confusing them for a partner/friend.

Added to this is the complexity of growing up in a household and feeling connected to your culture, but then constantly having to justify this to others outside of the home. Let's also not forget the intergenerational trauma that is passed down within families – this doesn't go away because you have lighter skin or look 'white'.

Proximity to whiteness allows many mixed-race people certain privileges and unless we recognise this and act upon it, we are continuing to uphold white supremacy. 'Passing' as white doesn't take away from your heritage, culture and lived experiences, but it *does* mean that you won't experience racism and structural racism in the same way as someone who is darker-skinned than you. Looking like a white person, but not feeling like one is complex.

The 2021 film, *Passing*, starring Tessa Thompson and Ruth Negga explores the relationship of two light-skinned Black women, Irene and Clare, the latter of whom lives her life 'passing' as a white woman. It's based on the 1929 novel of the same name written by Nella Larsen and was directed by actress Rebecca Hall. Interestingly, there was some initial criticism about the choice of director being a 'white woman' until it was revealed that Hall's grandfather was in fact Black but passed for white, meaning that her biracial heritage was often overlooked. After showing her mother the film Hall said:

> There were a lot of tears. [My mother] said that she felt her father would have been released by it on some level because he was never able to talk about it. This has given our family an ability to not feel like there's something that's hidden.[10]

The film was an incredibly interesting watch, and explored many of the nuances of colourism, including the chemistry between Clare and Irene's Black husband, Brian, and the insinuation they are having an affair. One of the most painful moments in the film occurs when the two women are reunited after many years and Clare introduces Irene to her white husband, John, played by Alexander Skarsgård, who has no idea that neither woman is white. Clare proceeds to encourage John to explain where her nickname 'Nig' originates, as the camera pans to the shocked face of Irene who must listen to his overt racism while maintaining her composure. What's also disturbing and tragically sad is Clare, who laughs along while giving knowing glances to her old friend as if to say, 'This is the choice I made and what I now have to live with.' It also begs the question: how many BIPOC have also had to sit through instances of their own white family spewing racist rhetoric?

~

We spoke to Yasmine* (she/her) who identifies as mixed race about what it is like to be considered 'white passing'.

Naomi and Natalie: What's your heritage and how do you identify?

Yasmine: I'm in my early twenties and my heritage is so hard to describe. My great-grandmother is from the Seychelles, a little island off the east coast of Africa. She met a Sri Lankan man in Kenya, they got married and had my nan; she's mixed race and is dark-skinned. Then my nan moved to the UK and met a white man, and she had my mum. My dad is white and that's how I'm white. So, I identify as mixed race: white and Black African.

Naomi and Natalie: Did you know much about your heritage and your culture growing up?

Yasmine: When you're a kid, you don't really see race, but when I was about six years old, I suddenly asked my mum one day, 'Mummy, why is nan Black? I'm so white and she is such a different skin colour. She's dark.' It was hard to believe that I came from her, and we have the same heritage.

Naomi and Natalie: How do people respond to you when you say you are mixed race?

Yasmine: When I say I'm mixed race to others, people always say, 'No you're not,' 'You have blue eyes and have straight hair,' (I straighten it) or, 'Your skin is white.' I used to get people asking me if I was Asian. I remember someone asked if I was half-Chinese. No one believes that my family is Black, so sometimes I say, 'Do you want to see a picture of

71

my family? Shall I show you a picture of my mum and my nan?' I felt really excluded from the Black community and from the mixed-race community, because I'm white passing. I feel like I'm fake. I feel like I'm not actually mixed race.

I have a brother who is darker-skinned. My mum said when I was born she was expecting me to have brown skin, thick curly hair and big brown eyes, and when I came out she said, 'Is that my baby?'

When my brother and I were at school, talking to each other or walking home together, people thought we were boyfriend and girlfriend. One time a classmate asked me, 'How is your boyfriend?' I said, 'I don't have a boyfriend – describe him.' The first word she said was 'brown'. I rolled my eyes and said, that's my brother: we are full siblings. In school, my brother would get called the n-word, he'd get called the C-word even though we're not Chinese. He would get so many horrible names for his skin colour, and I never got anything, even though we were full siblings. My mum told me that back when we lived in the US, when we applied for school, she put my race down as mixed race. I didn't get into the school. When she put me down as white, I got in. I was shocked. Alternatively, nowadays, if you say you're mixed race, on a job application or something like that, I feel like you're kind of more likely to get it because they want to look inclusive.

Naomi and Natalie: How do you feel about your identity now?

Yasmine: I remember one time in my life when I was really going through a lot of questioning and asking myself, 'Who am I?' and trying to figure out my heritage. I didn't understand why I looked so different. I have accepted who I am now. I don't really give it much thought anymore. I didn't even know there was a term for someone like me, who is mixed race, but is white passing. When I first heard that term,

I remember thinking, *That's me! I'm mixed race and I'm white passing.* So, I do definitely get more privileges than my brother does, which is so sad.

Jacob Seelochan (he/him) identifies as mixed race. He shared his experience of growing up believing he was of Brazilian heritage and discovering later in life he was actually Guyanese.

Natalie and Naomi: Firstly, how old are you? What's your heritage and where did you grow up?

Jacob: I'm Jacob and I'm in my mid-twenties. I was born and raised in Nottingham in the East Midlands and I'm Irish, Guyanese, Polish and English.

Natalie and Naomi: How did you find growing up mixed race in Nottingham?

Jacob: Well, I didn't identify as mixed race until I moved to London. I'd always just taken the time to explain my specific heritage to each new person. I didn't think that was unusual because I didn't know any other mixed-race people, no one identified as that in my area. I went to a Catholic school (which was a whole struggle in itself), and at the time there was a huge influx of Polish and Eastern European students. There was a lot of xenophobia in the news about Polish and Romanian immigrants 'taking British jobs', etc. and so I was never really the focus of any bullying or racism regarding my background. I slipped under the radar until mid-way through Catholic school, when my friends discovered that my dad was brown and half-Brazilian. (The discovery that he was actually Guyanese happened a lot later.) Then someone started a rumour that he was the head of the Brazilian mafia. Not only did it go through the kids at school, but the teachers also started saying it. One time my biology teacher overheard me telling a friend that my dad was out of town on a business trip, and she asked, 'What kind of business, though?' Now I look back at it, I don't know if that was OK or not because it was just such an odd thing to happen. I guess that was when I started to see my heritage a bit more in terms of how other people saw me. One story that always makes me laugh is there's this fair in Nottingham every October called the Goose Fair. It has a helter-skelter and a hook-a-duck and all that. One year I went with my group of friends from another school. We were all walking in a group when I realised that I was alone. I turned around to find them all a few feet behind me, looking at me. I said, 'What?'

They replied, 'We just noticed how big your butt is.' Then they said, 'It's probably because you're Brazilian.'

After that, it just became my thing – even my name in their phones was changed to 'Brazilian Butt'. It was so strange. When I went to college, a couple of them came with me, so that nickname stayed with me for a long time.

Natalie and Naomi: How did it make you feel at the time?

Jacob: Oddly enough I think at the time it made me feel empowered, because we're so distant from my South American family. I had never been given the words or the ammunition to understand that side of me, and that was the first time someone had vocally, externally and very obviously named that part of me. At the time I really felt validated and also as a young queer person, I felt sexually desirable for the first time. I felt like it was something that made me wholly unique in my friendship group. But over the past few years [getting through drama school and befriending lots more mixed-race people], I've realised that it may have done more harm than good. This stereotype of Brazilian people having curvy bodies and big behinds was: one, something I embraced, and the next: something I felt ashamed to have fed into. Acknowledging that this thing that made me feel powerful had also given permission to a group of white friends to continue stereotyping was really hard. And the added cringe of discovering my family's roots are Guyanese and not even Brazilian made for a real eye-opening experience.

Natalie and Naomi: Can you explain more about your Brazilian and Guyanese identity and why you grew up thinking that you were Brazilian?

Jacob: My identity journey has been frickin' wild. My parents weren't given the language to talk about it. I'm Guyanese, Irish, English and Polish. My English, Irish and Polish grandparents have been around my whole life; it's my Guyanese grandad that left before I was born. It's confusing having no connection to the part of me that made my skin this colour, that changed me from being white to mixed. My only access to that side of me is through the internet. We recently found out – through Google – that my grandad lives in Australia, and before that the United States, even though my dad had always been told his family resided in Brazil. We had never really gone digging. Recently, my older brother began finding people on Facebook with our surname, but spelt ever so slightly differently, and they were all from India or Guyana. So one day I just had a brave moment, added one of them and messaged saying, 'Hey, I don't know if you're my family or not, but my grandad is called [. . .] , do you know him?' And they replied, 'Yeah, he's my uncle.' We had a phone call and that's when we found out we're not Brazilian; we're Guyanese. Apparently, my great-grandparents moved to Brazil when they got more money because they needed to keep working, and there wasn't enough work in Guyana. They said the reason behind the different spelling of the surname is because they got stuck on the US border when they were trying to move to the States, so they had to change their surname to try again. This one cousin was able to map out an entire section of my family tree I'd never known before. What's so crazy to me was that this very easy hunting was never done before. I wonder if it was partly the fear of finding out something that would destabilise the already unstable lineage we have. Plus, my dad didn't really show an interest in that side of himself; I wonder if maybe because my grandad left my dad and grandma when they were very young. He was a trainee nurse, so I believe the story is that he would travel a lot and work in different countries. One time he left and said, 'I'm not coming back.' My cousin was shocked when I reached out because to them my grandad had always said he'd never have kids. In fact, this cousin was pretty sure he'd have no idea me and my siblings – his own grandkids – existed. My grandma didn't think it worth talking about much; it's the Irish Catholic in her. My family often referred to her ex-partner as 'he who must not be named'. But now that I've opened the door myself, I'm meeting these cousins and learning that my Guyanese family is intact and spread out across several continents! As a child, I thought my beige skin ended with my mysterious grandad, but it's kind of exciting to know I no longer have to rely on this person who wants nothing to do with me to complete my identity.

Natalie and Naomi: Growing up and knowing what you know now, how has that impacted you and your identity?

Jacob: Identity was never really a conversation when I was a kid. It only really became a conversation when I came to London. Drama schools are really trying to catch up with progressive identity politics and I think a lot of them are failing. There's a lot of very outdated practices behind those walls. One of those practices was fitting yourself into a neat and easily sellable box, ready for the white entertainment industry. That's where I learned to stop saying I was Guyanese-English-Irish-Polish and just say 'mixed race'. I became aware that explaining my heritage every time I met someone was 'too much'.

Natalie and Naomi: Had you not heard of the term 'mixed race' previously?

Jacob: I think the one time I did was when I was in Catholic school. I had this really close friend and we'd go for walks around the field every lunchtime; that was our routine. One time I must've said something about being mixed race and he said, 'You're not mixed race; you have to be half-Black and half-white to be mixed race.' I remember we had a bit of a debate about it and I never swung him round to my way of thinking. I guess that was my first experience of being denied my identity. I wonder if that experience of being completely shut down closed that term off to me, and it only returned to me in London out of necessity.

I've always really feared that moment when I meet a new person, and I see them thinking, *What is he?* in their heads. *Is he Indian? Mediterranean? Mixed? Latinx?* Some people don't even get that far – they just pass me off as white – but the worst feeling is not knowing what they've decided. That's when I feel at a disadvantage. I think that's why the term, 'white passing' has always been so confusing to me, because I've only ever been called white passing by white people. My friends who aren't white very rarely make that assumption. Their own experiences of being discredited because of their skin colour leads them to just asking and being more aware. So, to me, 'white passing' just feels lazy. It's a way of devaluing my experience because you were too lazy to see the complexity of race; you were stuck in the Black-and-white binary. Too many times I have changed how I identify because of other people's laziness.

Speaking of lazy assumptions, I'll never forget what happened back in Nottingham when I was in an amateur production of *Hairspray*. I played Link, who was one of the white leads in this musical about segregation. Just before one of the shows, one of the chorus members turned to me and said, 'You know, [. . .] told everyone you're way too Black to play Link.' I was so dumbfounded, because not only had this person never asked me about my background, but he was ignorant enough to recognise me as not being white and to decide I was Black. To him and a few other castmates, there was no in between.

Factors that will influence how you identify:

1. Who you have grown up with.
2. The area you have grown up in.
3. How your parents identified for you.
4. How you identify in other areas of your life.
5. What positive and negative experience you may have had with each parent.
6. What other people have called you.
7. What you feel most comfortable with.
8. How you feel the world views you.

As a mixed-race person, it is crucial that you interrogate where negative opinions of yourself have come from. Being honest about how you feel about yourself and allowing space to heal will enable you to help others and effect change. Perhaps you felt rejected by members of your family or community. Or do you hold internalised racism and anti-Blackness that needs to be addressed? Were negative or problematic things said to you in your past that you continue to believe about yourself? Have you been trying to please other people in order to be accepted? At the end of this book (see pp. 219–221), you will find resources and guidance which we hope will help you navigate and thrive in your identity, if these questions resonate with you.

We encourage you to look at the amazing positives of being mixed race. There is much to learn about ourselves. A sense of uniqueness. Cultures to explore. New relationships to build. Discovering more about ourselves can be both painful and liberating. Many of us are searching for places to belong, reconciling how we feel and how we move through the world. Ultimately, it is not until we start to accept the beautiful and more complicated parts of ourselves that we will ever start to feel comfortable in our own skin, but we must also accept it's unrealistic to be completely secure in our identity all the time.

If this resonates with you, take a deep breath and say to yourself:

'I am not alone.'
'There are others out there like me.'
'I am enough.'
'I have much to offer this world just as I am.'
'My experiences are valid.'
'No one has the right to erase my identity.'
'The pain I have experienced does not define my worth.'
'I have the right to choose my identity.'
'There is space for me to heal and grow.'

Chapter 4

'Do you tan?':

On navigating microaggressions

~~~

Natalie: Microaggressions, a term coined by Harvard University psychiatrist Chester M. Pierce in the 1970s, are usually understood as derogatory or hostile insults, general comments or behaviour directed towards marginalised groups. They target your race, gender identity, sexuality, ethnicity or your body (ableism).[1] Ultimately, they perpetuate the narrative that you are not accepted in the dominant group or in this case, the 'norm of whiteness'. They are often covert, so there are times when it's not even noticeable when they are being used, and they can be hard to identify or explain to someone who does not face the same type of discrimination. However, microaggressions are problematic enough that they can stop you in your tracks and leave you replaying a situation or words over and over in your mind. It can be difficult to challenge them, and if you do, more often than not, you are met with gaslighting (see p. 48).

Racial gaslighting is used to deny racism and undermine victims' experiences. Constantly having to explain your experience of racism and why it is racist undoubtedly has an impact on your mental wellbeing and self-confidence, as well as being exhausting. While the aggressor may feel it's harmless, microaggressions are often anything but. Ultimately, they are a way to 'other' people and, when it comes to racism, to ensure that whiteness remains the standard by which everything else is measured.

Microaggressions do not only come from overtly racist people who decide on a given day that they want to cause harm; they are also exhibited by those who would categorise themselves as 'nice' or 'good' and who maintain they wouldn't ever dream of saying anything racist. This is also why it can make you feel uncomfortable when you need to address it. Those who are unaware of microaggressions can react out of a place of shame or lack of understanding, and can, when challenged on their behaviour, become defensive. At times, microaggressions can even appear as a compliment, as some twisted way of giving you 'advice', or maybe even out of 'curiosity'. Whatever the reason, the result is the same: they continue to maintain and uphold white supremacy.

Microaggressions can be further split into three categories:[2]

Microassaults

Microassaults are explicitly discriminatory behaviour, although the person may not believe that their actions are harmful because they did not intend to be racist:

- 'I didn't know your dad was coloured.'
- 'I've got a really funny joke . . . [says racist joke].'
- 'That's because you're half-caste.'

Microinsults

Microinsults are a more subtle form of microaggression, in which people unintentionally communicate discriminatory messages to members of targeted groups:

- 'You don't look . . .'
- 'You're so exotic.'
- 'Can I touch your hair?' (Or, touching hair without asking.)
- 'I didn't think you were mixed race.'
- 'Is that really your mum/dad?'
- 'Stop acting like [insert racial group]. You're not.'

Microinvalidations

Microinvalidations deny the realities of what people really experience or exclude the feelings of marginalised people:

- 'I didn't expect your English to be so good.'
- 'Where are you *really* from?'
- 'I can't be racist; I have a mixed-race child/friend/partner/parent.'
- 'You are a real credit to your race.'
- 'Are you sure you haven't got any . . . in you?'
- 'You must be good at . . .' (Assumption based on race.)

For us, racial microaggressions have followed us around and are the most common way racism has shown up in our lives. When we were younger, we didn't have the language or the understanding to know what they were and although they would make us feel a certain way, we often brushed comments off as jokes or down to ignorance. What we have learned (the hard way) is that microaggressions can come from anyone and everyone, including friends, family, work colleagues, bosses, spiritual leaders, partners and so on. Being mixed race also means that you can experience these from family on both sides, something we discuss more in Chapter 6 (see pp. 124–139).

Naomi: One of the tools of white supremacy is the sense of ownership and authority over non-white bodies. There are often questions you have to endure that are less about curiosity and more about entitlement. Being mixed race also often means living with misconceptions about who you are because you're not always easy to 'categorise'. When I was pregnant with my first child, I suffered with hyperemesis gravidarum, a debilitating pregnancy condition, in which I was constantly sick and could barely eat. I would drive to work and have to pull over to be sick (that's if I could even get out of bed!). As a teacher this didn't work well, being in front of a class full of students! It was so extreme I had prenatal depression and in the end my mum took me to the doctor for help. I recall being sat in the office chair, head to the floor while she explained to him that I was extremely low and not coping with the hyperemesis. He looked at me and then looked across at my white, blonde-haired, blue-eyed mum.

'Are you adopted?' he asked, abruptly.

Through my nausea (which I can only describe felt like constant travel sickness), I glanced over to my mum who looked confused. 'Why are you asking that?', she replied.*

I remember how fragile I was physically and emotionally. I remember crying as Mum walked me home. Needless to say, I changed my doctor and was grateful I had my mum there to advocate for me. These sorts of microaggressions are everyday occurrences for marginalised people and they are anything but 'micro'. They build up. They play on your mind. They steal hours, days and weeks from you as you replay

---

*The issue here is not that I viewed adoption as an insult, but the assumption about my family set-up or the implication that my white mum couldn't be my biological mum was highly problematic.

them. They cause you to question who you are. They 'other' you and they can be traumatic. On top of that, when you try to explain this to white people, they will very often play devil's advocate and offer an explanation as to why it 'wasn't about race' or 'not meant to cause harm'. That's the thing about microaggressions: whichever way they play out, you lose.

Natalie: I remember sitting in a meeting at work. I was the only mixed-race person in my office and the only Person of Colour. I used to work for an events company and there were about six of us in the meeting talking about renaming some of the stages and venues for the event that year. We had a field that was known as the 'fete' because it had all the old school rides such as the Ferris wheel and the carousel. My boss used the word 'g*psy' during a sentence. I challenged him and said it's an ethnic slur and should not be used. While he accepted that, he then went on to say something along the lines of 'What can we say anymore?' It all happened so quickly, and the next thing I knew, my boss was saying the word 'n*****'. In context, he was explaining that they knew someone who was mixed race who would use the n-word in front of them. I got the sense that he viewed it all as 'banter'. While I was still trying to get my head around what was happening, he continued to say 'n*****'. I told him to stop and that he shouldn't be saying it, to which he responded, 'I am only repeating what he said.' Despite being extremely upset at this point, I proceeded to do what I'd been conditioned to do throughout my life: I prioritised the feelings of my white colleagues over my own. To offset the tension in the room, I stopped talking and pretended nothing had happened. I left the office that day and called my friend. I was conflicted, I wanted to talk to my sister and my mum because what had happened was such a massive thing, but I thought if I told them they would say I should leave my job; at the same time though, I was worried about not having a job. I cried and never spoke of it again until now. I call this incident a microaggression, but there was nothing about it that felt at all micro. The use of the word 'micro' feels like another way to discredit and diminish the feelings that these comments have on BIPOC.

~

In the study, 'You think you're Black?', which explores Black mixed-race people's experiences of Black rejection, Dr Karis Campion studies the concept of 'horizontal hostility' and explores the Black mixed-race identity, and how people can encounter inauthenticity from their Black counterparts.[3]

She explains that there has been a good attempt at introducing terminology when it comes to describing experiences of displacement, such as multiracial microaggressions, also known as racial invalidation. This means that sometimes there are specific microaggressions that mixed-race people experience. It also means that not only do mixed-race people experience racial microaggressions along with other BIPOC, but we also encounter our very own set of multiracial microaggressions targeted specifically at us. This results in being consistently reminded that we do not 'fit'.

An example of a multiracial microaggression is when someone assumes that you are monoracial. An example of this is someone saying something racist about Asian people in front of a white-passing Asian person who they assume is white and responding with something along the lines of, 'Oh well, you're different, aren't you?' or 'You don't even look it,' when the person corrects them or calls them out.

Denial about your experience is another way microaggressions show up for mixed-race people and can manifest in the form of someone deciding that you're not '[insert race here] enough' to really endure it or that the racism you experience could never be as potent as that of a monoracial person.

Other ways it can show up include people thinking that mixed-race people have 'identity issues', or that they must be 'so confused' because they haven't 'picked a side'. It's a way to make mixed-race people feel othered and as though they don't belong.

Naomi: March 2017 saw one of the most popular and funniest videos to circulate on the internet go viral.[4] Robert E. Kelly, a political science professor and respected academic, was being interviewed on BBC World News about the impeachment of South Korea's president when his daughter burst into his home office and proceeded to stomp around the room. She was quickly followed by her younger sibling and then by their mother, Jung-a Kim, who crawled into the room to try and usher the toddlers out of the room. Being a working parent of a confident four-year-old at the time I found it particularly funny and subsequently, working through lockdown with two children who would happily crash Zoom meetings at home, I could not empathise more with the situation. However, the video opened up another conversation due to the fact that many people assumed at the time that Jung-a Kim wasn't the partner of Kelly or mother of the children, but rather, the nanny. The assumption that she was the 'hired help' was rooted in stereotypes about Asian women and mixed-race relationships.

The tendency for people to make assumptions about whose children belong to whom came up a lot in our interviews. My mum told me people would outright ask her, 'Why is she so dark?' when they peered over the pram to take a look at the new baby she was pushing around. When I had my first son, I became friends with a white woman at the local baby group. Her (mixed-race) son was darker skinned than mine and when we went out together the assumption was always that her child was mine. As the boys grew, the assumptions continued unabated as one of the staff members at the local primary school they both attended presumed I was the parent of her son.

Ashton (he/him) identifies as Black mixed race. He spoke to us about the racism he faced growing up.

Naomi and Natalie: Could you tell us your name, your age, your heritage and where you grew up?

Ashton: My name's Ashton, I'm in my mid-twenties and my heritage is Jamaican and British. I identify as Black mixed race, just because I've been seen as Black my whole life. I grew up in a little town in north Norfolk. It's a small town and everyone is white country people. I grew up with just my mum, who is white, and my two sisters. My older sister is ten years older than me, so she moved when she was eighteen. So, it's been me, my mum, and my younger sister. My dad left when I was about four years old, and I've never had contact with him. My nan is around the corner, and she was very much a part of my childhood growing up. I didn't really have that much contact with the Black side of my identity when I was growing up. So that was even more of a challenge, especially being in a white-predominant area. There was no outlet for me to understand my identity. So now that I have grown up, I am learning that myself. I co-founded a project, 'Rewriting Rural Racism' in Norfolk because there was nothing for young people. I wrote a show about being mixed race in a rural area and I lead anti-racism workshops as well. I write a joke in the play that my mum tried her best to help me with my identity and she'd take me to the African drumming lessons [laughing] and I'm not even African. What's so funny is it was done at a private club, which was a Conservatives' club with old, middle-class white people – but I know she tried.

Naomi and Natalie: Could you share any times you have experienced racism or microaggressions growing up?

Ashton: My first experience was kids chasing after me calling me a chocolate bar, but the most predominant experience that's stuck with me forever is when I was playing football with my friend, who was my next-door neighbour, and his friend, who lived across the road. We were playing on the road, kicking the ball to each other. I was in Year 4 and he was in Year 6 and at the time it felt like such a massive age gap even though it was only two years. He started getting very rough with me and pushing me. He pushed me on the ground, pinned me on a car, pushed my head down and said to my friend, 'This is what they do to n******* in America.' I ran home crying. I told my mum, who informed the school, and [the boy] wasn't allowed to go on the school trips, but the fact that he was only ten years old and that came out of his mouth stuck with me.

Another incident was more indirect racism maybe, but we were reading *Of Mice and Men* at school. I had to read that in a room full of white students and I had no idea what the story was about. So, I was really shocked when the n-word was being mentioned in class, and the teacher didn't tell me this was going to happen. I said to the teacher, 'Can we stop reading this book as I don't feel comfortable being in class saying the n-word in front of everyone?' and the teacher said, 'This is what we're doing for our curriculum, so that's what we're going to do.' As I was a teenager, instead of articulating how I felt, I would just mess about in class because I was trying to distract from reading the book but then I got put in a different class. I just didn't want to read that book; it was just really insensitive of them to not even think about asking me. I've since written that part in my play, which is semi-autobiographical. I've spoken to people from other schools about the book. They have said to me that teachers say the n-word, but they say it shouldn't be used outside the classroom. I genuinely think that the book

91

shouldn't even be used at all. Other incidents that happened were general things like when I was younger people loved their golliwogs (which are children's toys made of soft material, usually in the form of a small man with a dark black face, stiff black hair and a large red mouth, now considered offensive to Black people). I remember being on a paper round and there would be golliwogs in people's windows. I knew that there was something wrong with that and I didn't even know what golliwogs were at the time, but I just knew that there was something odd about it. Other things where I would find myself in awkward discussions where people would forget that I'm mixed race and say things around me about other Black people or any other ethnic group, but because I've grown up with them, they thought I'd be fine with it and I guess because I'm mixed race, I'm 'not really Black, or whatever.'

Kym (she/her) and Courteney (she/her), both in their twenties, are sisters from Kent who spoke to us about their experiences of racism and racial microaggressions.

Naomi and Natalie: What is your heritage?

Kym and Courteney: Our mum is white (British English), and our dad is East Asian (of Chinese heritage). He was born in Malaysia and grew up there.

Naomi and Natalie: Tell us a little about your upbringing and whom you grew up with?

Courteney: We grew up in Kent with both our parents and then they split up when we were teenagers. I was fourteen and Kym was seventeen. Kym stayed with Dad and I lived with Mum. We lived in a very white area but had a lot of East Asians in our family. My mum's brother also married a Chinese–Malaysian woman.

Naomi and Natalie: Did you grow up with a lot of your British white family or did you grow up with a lot of your Malaysian family?

Courteney: We had Mum's parents around the corner who were white, but then we would go to Malaysia quite a lot growing up – at least once a year. Sometimes we went twice and there, we would see our grandfather, aunt, uncle and cousins. Our dad is quite private, so we didn't often meet his extended family or anything like that, so I would definitely say we spent more time with the white side of our family.

Kym: We have two cousins who are mixed race. They split their time between here and Malaysia. They probably were a lot more in touch with their Asian side because they went to an international school and their friends were Asian. Their mum spoke to them in Mandarin, and they had more of an Asian influence than me and my sister did.

Our dad was not so much into his culture and didn't massively educate us.

Courteney: I think a large part of it was that he wasn't around loads when we were kids; he worked a lot. He commuted to London every day for work. Most of my memories of my childhood are with my mum and then my dad coming home really late for dinner, and things like that. I think later in life, when we became teenagers, like late teens, he became a lot more present. He started working locally, and what with COVID and the increase of racism against East and South East Asians, we've had a lot more conversations with our dad about race. He wants us to be more in touch with our heritage now than he did when we were younger.

Naomi and Natalie: And do you think that's because you've become more educated as you have got older, that you're having these conversations with your dad?

Kym: I think we both do. I've said this before and it sounds really silly because I don't think about it now, but I never really saw myself as a different heritage in the sense of, I just thought because we didn't really talk about it personally, I didn't really think much of it. I just thought, *Oh, Dad's just from somewhere else*, and people would make comments about my dad, but I didn't really pay much attention. I mean, Courteney and I went to different schools. Courteney had a few more mixed-race friends, but I didn't have anyone else; everyone else was white, my friends are white. I just felt at the time people can just be a bit nasty, but now I'm a lot more aware of racism. I've never experienced seriously overt racism, more 'covert racism', which I used to say was just 'banter'. It did upset me, but I would never have brought it up to my dad.

Courteney: I don't think we ever spoke about it, to be honest.

Kym: I feel like we've only had conversations about it last year and Courteney has experienced stuff more recently. Looking back though, I remember one time I came home from school and told Mum that someone called me the C-word. The person did get expelled from school, but the thing is, I don't even know if [my mum] even knew what happened. When I did tell her things, her response would be something like, 'Oh, you know, that is not really a nice thing to say,' then we just didn't really talk about it. I don't think that she was trying to not broach the subject. I just don't think she understood.

Courteney: I don't know about you, Kym, but I think growing up I would have really valued the conversation about casual racism and the fact that it's not OK. Kym and I had a conversation last year where we ended up sharing a lot of experiences that we had – many of which I had no idea that she had experienced. Things that happened recently, like people saying, 'Oh, you're a little Asian girl.' We didn't talk to each other about it as kids, and people didn't talk to us about it either.

Naomi and Natalie: This is a bit more painful, but could you share examples of racist incidents or microaggressions that you have experienced, whether covert or overt?

Kym: At my workplace, an Asian colleague noted that they had financial issues due to COVID and someone else commented, 'Oh, well, they're the ones that started this, anyway!' Bearing in mind it's just us in the room. And then I was like, 'What do you mean?' And she said, 'You know, that probably sounds really racist, but what are you going to do about it?' I said, 'You can't say that because it's not true.' She just replied, 'But they're the ones that made us have this virus.' I said, 'No,' and noted she shouldn't talk like that. But I don't know whether they think I'm just white.

Courteney: I wonder whether she would have said that if you were of complete East Asian heritage, rather than mixed. I do think it's one of those situations where if you were to say back to her, 'Well, I am Asian,' you would get the classic reply of, 'Oh, well you're not really, though,' which is a very common response.

Kym: There are a lot of casually racist comments, like, if I've said, 'I don't really like rice,' someone might say 'But aren't you Asian?' and stuff like that. It's very difficult though, because when it's your superior, you can only say so much. It just puts you in a really awkward position sometimes when people are ignorant. I have had to correct people when they say words like 'oriental'. It makes me feel so uncomfortable. When I explain that you can't use those terms, people question me. Other examples of this are doing Chinese accents, using the C-word a lot more, taking the piss out of Asian

95

culture and making generalisations, like, 'Oh, you're Asian; you should know that.'

Courteney: I would just say the same, that I feel like we've hit home with the casual racism. I used to work in a supermarket and an employee there used to call me Lucy Liu. There was another East Asian woman who worked there, and I remember she was once compared to a Thai sex worker. We didn't really know how to respond.

Natalie: There is definitely a sense in the UK that we have a polite way of doing things and this manifests when it comes to racism. We're starting to gather the language and terminology around overt and covert racism. Did you find that you could talk to your parents about this?

Kym: I don't think I really even spoke to my dad about racism. Back in the day when I was at school, kids would say things about my dad and I was always too worried to tell him because I thought it would upset him, to the point that I didn't want him to collect me from school. I actually don't think my dad would have been upset about what the kids were saying; however, I felt bad on behalf of him. I think it [may have been] different for Courteney because she had more Asian friends.

Courteney: I did have more Asian friends, but I wouldn't say it reduced the amount of casual racism. We all had to deal with being 'othered' in some way, but we didn't really talk about it with each other. It was only really when we went to uni that we reconnected and realised how much casual and internalised racism we had endured. It's only in hindsight that I realise that me wanting to dye my hair blonde and using makeup to make my eyes look bigger was a way of me trying to Westernise my features. When you're surrounded by people who look a certain way, that's what you try to emulate.

But back to my dad; we didn't have personal conversations when we were younger anyway, so I didn't really feel like that was a space to have them. What I would have loved is if when we were younger, someone sat us down and said, 'Look, you're mixed race; this is a white area. People are probably going to say things. If they do, you should tell someone what they said.'

I have a memory from primary school. I went to the park with my friends and some of the guys said, 'Your dad is a Chinaman,' and other racist things. I reported it to the head teacher, and he said, 'I'm going to do something about this.' Nothing was ever done. All the teachers in our school were white. I wonder, how much at that time did they really understand about racism? How much can they understand that these words really affect you and can manifest into internalised racism. The teachers didn't understand at the time. I'm not sure what it's like now.

In 2017, I was in Embankment Gardens. At the time, I was doing an internship and because it was unpaid, I worked some evenings. So, I had these small periods to eat some dinner and then go to work. That day I was eating in the gardens minding my own business when this guy came over. He just sort of slid over, said, 'Hey,' and started chatting me up. I was polite and explained I was not interested, which pissed him off, but he didn't move. I explained again that I didn't want to chat and then he got angry and said I was lucky he didn't spit on my face. He walked away to sit with these two other guys who I don't think he actually knew. It seemed to me as if they were scared of him, to be honest. I thought it was over, but he started yelling things like, 'You look like you have anorexia,' and then he clocked I was mixed race and he started making racist comments, saying, 'You're disgusting. You're half-Chinese. Look, she is disgusting, she looks like the girl from *The Ring*.' He just wouldn't stop. It made me really sick. I was scared, and I remember these two women were nearby, yelling at him to shut up, but everyone else kept their heads down. In the end I called the police, but when I explained the situation and the overt racism to the police officer, he said that the man sounded like 'a really bad flirt', that I probably bruised his ego by rejecting him.

The second incident was more recently, just before Christmas. I was playing badminton with my friend who is also of East Asian heritage. This guy came over and started watching us playing. There were other people on the court, other girls. My friend said something to me, and he shouted, 'What did you say to me?' My friend explained that she wasn't talking to him. I felt uncomfortable, so I suggested we leave. We went to the changing rooms, got changed and I remember feeling like this guy wanted trouble. I was on edge and it was dark outside. When we left, I saw him. He had been waiting for us. We walked really quickly, and I looked back and he wasn't moving, so I thought, *OK, he isn't following us, that's good.* The next thing I know, he's on his bike trying to run us over and we were walking on the pavement and he's basically just trying to ram us down with his bike. Then he stopped in front of us, turned back and tried to do it again. It was so scary. We started running and he began circling us and yelling abuse. None of the restaurants or shops nearby were open, so there was nowhere safe to run to. Then he started saying, 'You're disgusting, I want to see you scared,' and spat on me. I felt targeted, because there were other girls on the court, but he was obsessed with us from the start. We managed to run to a cafe that was open, and we called the police. Again, they were nice, and they took our statements, but ultimately claimed they were unable to access CCTV footage at the gym, since it would be closing for Christmas. We didn't hear anything after that. Hate crimes against East Asians during COVID have tripled since last year and I feel like it's really tainted my experience of London. I just feel unsafe. When your race is called out and people say how disgusted they are by you, it makes you feel really awful.

~~

The word 'microaggressions' is now widely used but for some can be misleading particularly in the use of the word 'micro' when the impact is anything but. As Ibram X. Kendi says:

> I do not use 'microaggression' anymore. I detest the post-racial platform that supported its sudden popularity. I detest its component parts – 'micro' and 'aggression.' A persistent daily low hum of racist abuse is not minor. I use the term 'abuse' because aggression is not as exacting a term. Abuse accurately describes the action and its effects on people: distress, anger, worry, depression, anxiety, pain, fatigue, and suicide.[5]

Microaggressions can be likened to mosquito bites. One bite can be painful enough for you to notice it's there because it hurts or itches, but it's not enough to stop you from going about your day-to-day; it's extremely frustrating. However, if you get bitten multiple times a day, it's going to start taking its toll and affecting you. When you're at work, the itchiness might distract you; it might become hard to concentrate on what's in front of you because you can't stop thinking about the pain and discomfort you're feeling. Now, instead of it being bites, replace that feeling with the everyday racial microaggressions you may experience. Why is it that you're expected to get on with your day? Microaggressions, along with overt racism should be challenged at every corner. Of course, there will be times where it just isn't safe to call it out, or moments where you don't feel confident to do so because it's traumatic.

Here, we're going to give you some practical tips on how to handle multiracial microaggressions when they arise.

How to deal with microaggressions:

- Microaggressions can sometimes take you by surprise. You may need a moment to reflect on what actually just happened. It may be helpful to speak to someone you know and trust who you can talk it through with. Someone who will listen and who understands how microaggressions show up.
- You will then need to think about how you want to respond. This will depend on a number of factors. For example, will you be safe if you respond in the moment? Do you need to do it in person or is there another way you could communicate your feelings? Is it best to wait, so that you can write down what happened and its impact? Do you need someone else with you for support?
- When speaking to people who have used inappropriate language or made offensive statements, it's often helpful to use the word 'I', for example, 'When you said ____ I felt like ____'. It's more difficult to argue with someone's actual feelings.
- If you are in the workplace, you may need to go and speak to your HR (Human Resources) department or the inclusion team to raise your concerns. If it's an ongoing issue, keep a log about what has been said, so you are able to provide evidence.

Of course, in the moment, we're not always going to respond in the most productive way, especially if we are feeling angry or betrayed. Not every situation plays out into a neat scenario and it may be that we need some more concrete strategies in place if we find it difficult to process or manage our emotions. The unfortunate reality is that as BIPOC we are going to face microaggressions at some point in our lives.

Excuse me, your microaggression is showing – how to respond if someone challenges you

Natalie: We all hold prejudices and biases. I have definitely caused harm to other minority groups out of ignorance and biases, whether it was using homophobic words as a teenager, misgendering, or not challenging people when hearing offensive language. It wasn't until I was older and actively read more and listened to what the LGBTQ+ community were saying that I realised how homophobic and transphobic comments might show up. Conscious and unconscious bias is in all of us, but we must learn to interrogate it and take responsibility when we are challenged, or realise we have caused harm. Being mixed race does not make you immune from this. If someone challenges you on something you've said, try not to become defensive. It's not easy if you feel ashamed or embarrassed, but it's important to remember that we don't always understand the impact of our words and when someone challenges us it can be just as difficult for them to say it as it is for us to hear it.

Some phrases to use in response if you are challenged:

1. 'Thanks for bringing that to my attention; it's something I didn't realise, and I need to find out more about that.'
2. 'I'm sorry for making you feel that way; I recognise this is something I need to try and understand better.'
3. 'I have never thought about it that way; I appreciate you taking the time to speak to me about it.'
4. 'Is there anything I can do/change in order to ensure I don't repeat this mistake?'

Chapter 5

'You're not like the others':

On light-skinned privilege

~~

Naomi and Natalie: In October 2019, Oscar-winning actress Lupita Nyong'o gave an interview to BBC *Newsnight* to discuss her new children's book, *Sulwe*,[1] the story of a young girl who has darker skin than the rest of her family. Speaking on the book, Lupita stated: 'I definitely grew up feeling uncomfortable with my skin colour because I felt like the world around me awarded lighter skin.'

Lupita Nyong'o was born in Mexico and grew up in Kenya, where she experienced those with lighter skin gaining preferential treatment. The roots of colourism are intrinsically linked to racism and enslavement, when lighter-skinned enslaved people were given preferential treatment because of their proximity to whiteness.

~~~

In eighteenth-century Jamaica, enslaved people outnumbered their enslavers by one to eight. This meant that enslavers sought to find ways to retain their power to avoid any uprising. One way in which to guarantee this would not happen was to ensure a colour hierarchy existed in which whiteness was at the top, followed by those with lighter skin – many of whom were known as 'mulattoes'. The word 'mulatto' derived from the Spanish word for 'mule' was used to identify mixed-race people. The term would commonly refer to someone who had African and European ancestry and were often the offspring of Black enslaved women who were raped and abused by their enslavers. It is believed that between 1850 and 1860 the 'mulatto' slave population increased by 67 per cent.[2]

According to the 1861 autobiography, *Incidents in the Life of a Slave Girl* by Harriet Jacob:

> *Southern women often marry a man knowing that he is the father of many little slaves. They do not trouble themselves about it. They regard such children as property, as marketable as the pigs on the plantation; and it is seldom that they do not make them aware of this by passing them into the slave-trader's hands as soon as possible, and thus getting them out of their sight.*[3]

Laws in Virginia stated that white women who gave birth to 'mulatto' children faced five years of servitude themselves and thirty years for the child. Having a lighter skin tone would often determine where you would work on a plantation, and often these lighter-skinned women were chosen to work in the house, rather than out in the field. In his 1861 book, *The Cotton Kingdom*, Frederick Law Olmsted wrote:

> *The mulattoes are generally preferred for in-door occupations. Slaves brought up to house-work dread to be employed at field-labour; and those accustomed to the comparatively unconstrained life of the negro-settlement, detest the close control and careful movements required of the house-servants.*[4]

When we talk about enslavement, we often hear about how light-skinned people had a 'better' existence because of their proximity to whiteness. It is true that lighter skin provided better opportunities – lighter-skinned people were more likely than darker-skinned people to be released from enslavement. Following abolition, many lighter-skinned women benefited from belonging to higher social and economic statuses than darker-skinned women, within a colour class-system that still exists today. However, it is important to remember the complexities and the very real horrors that they experienced.

Regardless of their position, these women were still enslaved and subjected to torture, rape, murder and other brutalities. Added to this was the complex issue that much of the abuse being carried out was by the people they were biologically related to.

The Blue Vein Society

After enslavement, disparity in the treatment of Black people continued based on skin tone. At the turn of the century clubs were formed by lighter-skinned Black people called 'Blue Vein Societies'. Only those whose skin was light enough to visibly see the blue veins beneath it were admitted.[5]

The brown paper bag test

The 'brown paper bag test' was historically used in the United States during the twentieth century to determine certain privileges a person would be afforded. A brown paper bag would be held against the skin of Black and brown people to decide whether their skin was lighter or darker than the bag.

The test was a notable example of a once-common form of prejudice. Access to social events, jobs, clubs, and schools was often determined by a person's complexion. According to Georgetown sociology professor Michael Eric Dyson, 'New Orleans invented the brown paper bag party – usually at a gathering in a home – where anyone darker than the bag attached to the door was denied entrance.'[6]

Colourism continues to impact many countries across the world, particularly those who were colonised by Europe. Having lighter skin and an aesthetic proximity to whiteness can offer social advantages. It's important to note, however, that these experiences are nuanced and can differ for mixed-race people depending on multiple factors, including skin tone as well as hair texture and facial features.

In the nineteenth century, white women would go to painful extremes, using powder, paint and even arsenic complexion wafers, to achieve a fairer complexion.[7] The preference for having pale skin came from the notion that higher-class and wealthy women did not work. Having darker skin was associated with lower classes, manual labour and those working outside, thus, their skin being darkened by the sun. European standards of beauty remain the hallmark from everything we see in fashion, beauty, film and beyond.

Nothing illustrates this more than the lucrative skin-bleaching industry. On 3 June 2020, Unilever – the multinational company that owns beauty-care product companies Dove and Pond's – posted the slogan, 'We have a responsibility for racial justice' on their Instagram page.[8] They were met with hundreds of comments questioning why the company that owned 'Fair & Lovely', a skin-lightening cosmetic sold mainly in Asia, were professing their commitment to anti-racism, yet at the same time selling products to lighten skin tones.

After much backlash, later that month the company announced that Fair & Lovely would be renamed 'Glow & Lovely'. In the same month, L'Oréal announced they would remove the words such as 'fairness' and 'whitening' from their products, some of which were also specifically marketed as skin-whitening products in South Asian countries. At the same time, matchmaking site Shaadi.com, a network that is predominantly frequented by South Asian people, announced they would be removing their skin-tone filter, which allowed users to search for potential partners based on how light or dark their skin was. Indian film actors such as Priyanka Chopra wrote in support of the movement, 'There is so much work to be done and it needs to start at an individual level on a global scale. We all have a responsibility to educate ourselves and end this hate.' Despite this, she was criticised for having previously endorsed skin-lightening products and not acknowledging the connection between colourism and racism.[9]

Skin-bleaching is a global phenomenon and a billion-dollar industry, so while companies under pressure are willing to rebrand, the practice will not cease unless consumers stop buying these products. Skin lightening works by reducing the amount of melanin or production of melanin in the skin. Many products are sold illegally as they contain chemicals, such as hydroquinone, that are considered dangerous. Serums, creams and soaps that contain mercury can hinder the development of melanin, which can have serious consequences and lead to kidney damage, rashes and scarring, not to mention the psychological impact.

In 2019 actress, presenter and activist Jameela Jamil, who is of South Asian heritage, spoke out about having been airbrushed at the start of her career to appear to have lighter skin and the problems with skin whitening among people in her community. 'The discrimination in my own culture against our natural beautiful brown skin is disgusting,' she said. 'Bleaching and whitening creams should be banned.'[10]

The fact is that whiteness has been upheld as synonymous with success, virtue and opportunity, and as BIPOC it has often been the case that the closer you are to whiteness, or the more you emulate it, the easier it becomes to move through the world.

So how does colourism manifest in today's society?

- Studies have shown that there is a wage gap linked to those who are dark-skinned and light-skinned.[11]
- Light-skinned Black women are more likely to be married than their darker-skinned counterparts.[12]

- The skin-lightening industry is estimated to reach a valuation of $24 billion (£19 billion) in the next decade.[13]
- Representation of light-skinned and mixed-race people over dark-skinned people in the media (and when there is representation of darker-skinned women it often perpetuates racist stereotypes such as the 'angry Black woman').[14]
- Makeup and accessories (tights, underwear, etc.) not being suitable for darker skin tones.
- Dark-skinned Black defendants are twice as likely as light-skinned Black defendants to get the death penalty for crimes involving white victims.[15]
- Preference for light-skinned models on the front covers of magazines.[16]

In her 2016 TEDx Talk 'Confessions of a D Girl: Colorism and global standards of beauty',[17] which has been viewed over a million times, Chika Okoro (addresses colourism in the entertainment industry using the example of a casting call posted on the Sande Alessi Casting company Facebook page for the Universal Pictures production, *Straight Outta Compton*. The recruitment for female actors was broken down into four categories from A–D. The 'A' girls were described as the 'hottest of the hottest' and the 'D' girls were described as 'African-American girls. Poor, not in good shape. Medium to dark skin tone'. The studio released a statement stating that they didn't approve or condone the information in the casting notice and Sande Alessi apologised for their offensive language,[18] but these examples reinforce the overwhelming bias placed on light-skinned and mixed-race actors as more desirable examples of beauty.

In 2018, Beyoncé's father Dr Mathew Knowles gave an interview to the radio station BBC Radio 5 Live, in which he highlighted the problem with record companies and radio stations perpetuating colourism:

This is the record industry and the music industry that has chosen to have this colourism, because in America you can't name in the last ten years . . . [there's] maybe one person in the last ten years that wasn't a lighter shade of black at pop radio. It's a 100 per cent fact.

In his book, *Racism From The Eyes of a Child*, he recounts the horrendous racism he and his family experienced growing up in 1950s Alabama, as well as his own encounters with colourism. He recounts some experiences with his mother, noting, 'She never wanted me to bring home or date someone that [had a] dark complexion.'[19]

Being lighter skinned can also allow access to places and opportunities not given to those with darker skin, and it's a notion that can be upheld within People of Colour's own families. The 2002 film *Bend it like Beckham* follows Jesminder Bhamra, or 'Jess' (played by Parminder Nagra), a British-Indian girl who is exploring her identity while balancing her parents' expectations. Her mother is angry with her for playing football and criticises her for playing outside, scolding, 'Look how dark you've become playing in the sun!'[20]

Meghan Markle and colourism
A recent moment when the conversation about light-skinned privilege came to the forefront of the media was after Harry and Meghan's infamous interview with Oprah Winfrey. On 7 March 2021 CBS aired a two-hour-long interview in which Prince Harry and Meghan, Duchess of Sussex, discussed their reasons for leaving royal life in the UK and relocating to Los Angeles. Meghan revealed that there had been concerns and discussions about how dark their son Archie's skin might be when he was born, with Harry also revealing that their decision to leave the UK was also, in part, down to the racism from the tabloids.

Meghan discussed the impact of the situation on her mental health and how it led to her having suicidal thoughts. With the trauma of racism all too familiar for so many Black and brown people, there was much support for Meghan from the community, with many Black women in particular on TV and in the media acknowledging their lack of surprise, and even recounting similar situations in their own families. As one Twitter user, @esthergbenz, wrote: 'Colourism is what allowed Meghan to marry into the Royal Family and anti-black racism is what forced her out of it.'

Meghan was, however, in many ways the most agreeable and tolerable form of Black person. Featurism, texturism and colourism play a part here – with her light skin and straight hair, Meghan was seen, by Eurocentric standards, as 'palatable' and 'acceptable'. Yet, her experiences show that she was still not considered white 'enough' to be accepted as a 'true royal' by the public or by some sections of the British Royal family. Anyone with an understanding of the history of the monarchy and the British Empire will know that white supremacy is the bedrock on which it is built, therefore, to think that racism would not be an issue is to lack understanding about how colourism even works.

Fetishisation

Colourism also shows up through racial fetishism, with light-skinned or mixed-race women being deemed to have 'the best of both worlds'. Many mixed-race women we spoke to shared their experiences of feeling like they were being used as an experiment, a way for white people who have never dated non-white people to have an 'exotic' experience. Colourism can also manifest within romantic and intimate relationships and notions of desirability. The narrative of lighter-skinned women being the ideal is one that is still upheld in many industries, notably the music industry. There are a plethora of songs which demonstrate a preference for white, mixed-race and light-skinned Black women, and uphold their beauty as superior to that of darker-skinned Black women, from Jay-Z's 'December 4th' to studio footage of Kodak Black's rapping about wanting 'yellow bones' and not wanting any 'Black b*tch'. In 2016 Kanye West caused outrage when he invited only 'multi-racial women' to a casting in New York for his Yeezy fashion show. People quickly took to Twitter to call out his casting call, tweeting comments like: 'Kanye West asking for multiracial models kind of sends an anti-Black message.'[21]

While 'multiracial' does not mean you cannot be dark-skinned, many interpreted the call-out as 'light-skinned women only'. Kanye later explained in an interview with *Vogue* that the wording for the casting call came following a conversation with his collaborator: 'How do you word the idea that you want all variations of Black?'

In July 2020 Lil Wayne's daughter, Reginae Carter, hit back at his interview with 50 Cent on Young Money Radio (Apple Music), in which both made offensive and derogatory comments about Black women, referring to them as 'exotic' and 'angry'.[22] There has also been much conversation around the casting of predominantly mixed-race and light-skinned Black women in hip-hop videos, and how this reinforces colourism. It's not only the music industry where we see this play out. There have been numerous examples of colourism in operation within the fashion industry and the digital lightening of celebrities and models in magazines. In the October 2010 *Elle* issue, the photograph of Oscar-nominated actress Gabourey Sidibe's skin was noticeably lighter than in other photographs[23] and actress Freida Pinto's photographs for L'Oréal also appeared to make her look distinctly lighter-skinned.[24] In 2015 *Style* was accused of whitewashing the front cover featuring actress and producer Kerry Washington, and images of Willow Smith and Zendaya on the front of *W* caused outrage when readers accused the publications of lightening their skin. Both magazines defended these, citing 'lighting' issues, as opposed to intentional lightening of the skin.[25] The fact remains that when there is representation of BIPOC you are far more likely to see light-skinned and mixed-race people front and centre.

'Blackfishing' is a term that came into the mainstream through a Twitter thread by the journalist Wanna Thomson in 2018. The thread started with: 'Can we start a thread and post all of the white girls cosplaying as black women on Instagram? Let's air them out because this is ALARMING'.[26]

Blackfishing is used to describe white people who appear to imitate the look and style of Black or mixed-race people in order to appear racially ambiguous.[27] It can show up in different forms, but some of the main ways are darkening skin or using excessive tanning products, having cosmetic surgery to appear Black or mixed race, i.e., making your lips or bottom bigger, cultural appropriation of hairstyles i.e., box braids or locs, using Photoshop to alter features or using makeup to deliberately appear racially ambiguous. The reason blackfishing is so problematic is because it's another way that white people can profit from Black bodies. Black people and POC have often had to assimilate to white standards, while blackfishing enables white people to pick and choose parts of being Black without facing any of the racism that comes with it.

Natalie Morris, author of *Mixed/Other* and a journalist for *Metro* recently wrote an article called 'Mixed-fishing'. What's interesting about this term is it identifies those people who are trying to look 'Black' but connecting more to the Black mixed-race aesthetic. A more recent example of this was when artist Jesy Nelson released the music video to her song, 'Boyz'. She came under a lot of scrutiny for 'mixed-fishing' by over-tanning, plumping up her lips and utilising styles in her music video associated with hip-hop music. Natalie argues that 'Ethnic smudging' may be a better way to convey the subtlety and nuance that is actually happening in cases like this one – the way racialised features, skin tone and body types seem to be manipulated and used in a way that ultimately reaffirms racial hierarchies.'[28]

Diversity is not a tick-box exercise and just because a Person of Colour is present, it does not mean colourism and racism are not at work. Of course, we must remember those at the intersections of discrimination. While light-skinned, mixed-race people will have advantages because of their skin tone, there will also be those who face other forms of prejudice, such as ableism, homophobia and transphobia.

If you are a light-skinned, mixed-race person, how do you ensure you are not perpetuating colourism or erasing darker-skinned people and the most marginalised people within that group?

- Scrutinise your own conscious and unconscious bias. Are there areas in which you have been harbouring anti-Blackness or colourist attitudes?
- Acknowledge how you have benefited from privilege and the difference in experience. Look at who is and isn't in the room. Are you taking up space that should be passed over to, or include, others?
- Be prepared to challenge when you see colourism in operation.

Isla (she/her) is a primary school teacher. She is in her mid-thirties and was born in Scotland, lived in Germany and Italy and now lives in England. She shares her experiences of learning about colourism.

Isla: My name is Isla. I identify as Black mixed heritage. I sometimes use the word 'mixed race', but I prefer not using the word race. It just depends on the conversation and where I am. My mum was Black Jamaican, and my dad was white Scottish.

Natalie and Naomi: Could you let us know a bit about where you grew up – who was in your family home and what the surrounding area was like?

Isla: I was born in Scotland. My parents met in Rome, which is somewhere we also lived when I was quite young. We moved between Germany and Italy when I was really young. Then I went to primary school in Germany. For the most part, I was the only Black or brown child in my section because it was a European school. We had different European sections; I was in the English section. I remember very clearly that the French section seemed to have lots of Black and brown students, but the English section didn't, and I was treated accordingly. We moved when I was ten, to Kent in England, which is a very white area and always was, up until more recent years. I've sort of moved away and come back again. I moved after my A levels; I went to the Dominican Republic for a year and that was amazing because it's a Caribbean island and the history is very, very mixed, so I blended in very well, which was like a completely new experience for me. Being anonymous was amazing. It was really wonderful, and I really found my voice and I found myself in many ways. Then I moved to London for uni, moved back, moved away, moved back again and now I currently live in Kent.

Natalie and Naomi: Looking at your childhood, what were your experiences like as a child of mixed heritage?

Isla: I actually can't put a finger on when I first noticed my mixedness because I don't think I was always aware of it. I could obviously see that my parents were a different colour, but they were my parents and I just absolutely saw them in that way and didn't differentiate racially between them. It may surprise many people to know that we didn't suffer a huge amount of racism in Germany. There are a couple of very distinct experiences that I do remember, for example, a group of young men walking past us and shouting the German equivalent of the n-word, at my mum. Then on a train, a drunk, middle-aged white man got on and he was insistent that we should stand up to let him sit down when there were other people without children. I remember it being a really uncomfortable situation. They sound quite few, and I think maybe this is because I was young and a bit oblivious. I'm sure my mum, being dark-skinned, experienced far more than I was aware of. Moving to Kent in England, it was much the same. To be honest, there wasn't loads of overt racism, but if I think back about it with my thirty-six-year-old head on, actually there were some occasions where we experienced racism.

Natalie and Naomi: Did you ever have that conversation with your mum or dad about anything to do with racism?

Isla: We did, but I think my mum was quite keen to assimilate, I suppose. She moved from Jamaica when she was only twelve, and my grandparents at the time were very eager to get by, make their fortune and a home here, which they ended up doing successfully. Whereas for some other families, I think their intention was to make some money and go back home again. I think they [my family] were quite happy to sort of settle here. The idea of fitting in was quite important. My mum lost her accent pretty quickly and so did my aunt. My grandparents never did, but they were older. There was that kind of attitude of being 'the good immigrant', and that was definitely the way that they functioned. I think my mum had carried that on to a certain extent, though not fully. She never relaxed her hair; she always had an Afro. She was very outspoken about things in her workplace, she worked in schools with children with physical disabilities and there were a lot of children who were placed at the school from London, which meant there were quite a lot of Black children, and their skincare and hair care was not thought about. So, my mum championed that, and it really pissed a lot of people off and, to this day, if I bump into people that she worked with, they will always say, 'Oh, you know, she did know her own mind,' and I would think, *Well yeah, good*, but she was clearly seen as overstepping the mark a little. We did have a conversation about race, but they took the form of life discussions. I also had these conversations with my dad, who was white. I remember having talked with him about my school in Germany and how I was treated by a number of teachers, and I hadn't ever attributed their treatment of me to my race. I can now obviously see that that is definitely what it was and having read Akala's *Natives*, he talks a lot about his experience in primary school and about how he was put into remedial classes because the teachers didn't know what to do with him. That's very much my experience. I wasn't badly behaved and I wasn't intellectually challenged. But I got the blame for most things.

Natalie and Naomi: Sometimes being mixed race means we have lighter skin, and we have light-skin privilege. When and how did you learn about colourism?

Isla: I remember an incident that always stays with me. At the time, I was a teenager. I just hadn't processed it; I didn't understand what happened. I remember going into my mum's workplace with her and one of her managers said, 'Oh, well, your daughter's more beautiful and more attractive than you are, isn't she?' I remember my mum being really offended and me being a bit awkward, thinking, *Oh, that was a compliment*, but in a really weird way. Why do I feel upset about that? I wasn't able to process it at that moment. Obviously, my mum being my mum said, 'Ohhhh, thank you' but clearly was hurt by what he said. It wasn't until later on that I realised he was basically saying, 'Oh, look, your daughter's not as dark as you are. Good for her.' That still stays with me now.

I don't think there was ever one moment where I suddenly learned about colourism. I think it was a drip-feed situation, a process where there were things that would happen over the course of years and it would then form a full picture. It's a bit like a puzzle. I'd get one piece every couple of years, like the situation that I mentioned with my mum and her workplace, and then piece them together.

One really big part of the puzzle was when I was in the Dominican Republic. Skin colour is a huge thing there and they've got terms that describe your shade of brown that ranges from white to black. For example, white was *blanca* or *blanco*; between that is called *india*, which is what they describe me as, which I think referred more to my features than necessarily my complexion, although my complexion would be in keeping with that, probably too. Then there's *triguena*, which is oats or wheat. Then there's *prieto*, which is a slightly derogatory term meaning really dark. That was a real visceral encounter with colourism because, as with many Caribbean and Latin American countries, you can very visually see the hierarchy according to the colour of your skin. If you go to a bank or shop, everyone front of house is light-skinned and back of house, everyone's darker. I remember expressing my pride in being Black and my mum being from Jamaica and the response was, 'Oh, you don't need to talk about that part of you.' I think it's definitely changed because this was almost twenty years ago when I was there first, although colourism has got worse because there's a large Haitian community and Haitians are generally very dark-skinned Black people and so the Haitian community are facing much more mistreatment. However, there's been a lot of progress around the natural hair movement and embracing African heritage, rather than only acknowledging European Spanish and Indigenous Taíno Indian influences. More Afrocentric narratives have started to emerge in the Dominican Republic.

So, I realised this is a real thing; I was being treated better than my African American friend. When I went back a second time to the Dominican Republic, I was studying, and I befriended a few Americans and there was one friend in particular who was dark-skinned and was treated very differently to the way I was treated. I think for me, where I do hold power and there's an opportunity for me to pass the mic or allow someone else to do the talking, then I try to stay conscious of that and try and make sure that that happens. I know that I'll always make mistakes. I think it's an interesting thing to accept your privilege, because when you tick a couple of boxes of marginalisation, it's quite difficult to think, 'Do I have any privilege at all?' but there really is, in a different way. I think there's so much to be unpicked. I don't claim to speak for anyone else, unless someone has exactly the same experiences and circumstances as I do. When I've been part of discussions in recent years, I've always tried to acknowledge that my experience as a Black woman is this. I appreciate and acknowledge that my experience is coming from a place of privilege as a light-skinned person, so I try to stay aware and as conscious of that as possible.

Reflections:

1. Where have you experienced preferential treatment because of your proximity to whiteness?
2. Have there been occasions when you have taken up space which should have been passed over to darker-skinned people?
3. How has your anti-racism work centred lighter-skinned people at the expense of darker-skinned people?
4. Where have you thought about, or treated dark-skinned people differently to those with light skin?
5. What parts of this chapter have challenged or triggered you? Are there areas where you need to interrogate your responses further?

As you finish reading this, it is important to note we included this chapter because we know we directly benefit from colourism and light-skinned privilege. We encourage you to take your learning about colourism from those who are most negatively impacted by it and whose voices must be centred in this conversation. We ourselves are still learning and unpacking our own fragility when it comes to colourism; therefore, while we knew we needed this chapter in the book, it is the people who face the most marginalisation who we must be listening to. This will be an ongoing learning journey for many of us.

Chapter 6

'Stop using the race card!':

On racist family members

Natalie: It was 8 a.m. on a Tuesday morning in May. I reached over to the side of my bed and picked up my phone like I do most mornings. I opened up my messages and saw an image my uncle had sent me on social media. I clicked on it. It was a meme depicting a picture of a white beauty queen with long blonde hair and a sparkling tiara. In her hands she was holding up a giant placard.

The sign read: **'Stop using the race card!'**

We can only assume that my uncle's message was in response to us starting our Everyday Racism account and the increase in the news and social media posts about the BLM (Black Lives Matter) movement. We didn't engage. We told our mum, and she took up the difficult conversation with him, telling us, 'It's not your responsibility to address this with him.'

The title of Reni Eddo-Lodge's book, *Why I'm No Longer Talking to White People About Race*[1] is incredibly powerful and marks a very significant change in the way people around us started to talk about race. This book was a big game-changer for us personally. Finally, someone had articulated how we had felt growing up in the UK. We were able to process our experiences in more depth, and we found great comfort in knowing a lot of what we felt about existing in a white-majority society was completely valid. The book opened up conversations that we had never seen before. However, the recurring question we had was, 'What if you can't just stop talking to white people about race, because white people are your family and, for some, your only family?'

125

Racism in your home

The racism mixed-race children can face from their own families, particularly in the cases of those who have white family members, is something that is not acknowledged or discussed enough. From dealing with a racist uncle at Christmas and experiencing microaggressions from your own parents to even facing rejection, being mixed race means you may face racism from those who are supposed to be your support network. This is undoubtedly one of the things that makes the experience of being mixed race a complex one. According to a Pew study conducted in 2015, the racism towards mixed-race people from their own family members differs according to their racial heritage.

While some multiracial adults report limited contact with certain racial groups in their family, relatively few say that they've been treated badly by family members because of their mixed-race background. Overall, 9 per cent of multiracial adults say that a relative or member of their extended family has treated them badly because they are mixed race. Nine in ten say this has not happened to them.

Some multiracial groups are more likely than others to say they have had this type of experience. Among biracial adults who are white and black, 21 per cent say they have been treated badly by

a relative because of their mixed-race background. And 19 per
cent of multiracial adults who are white, black and American
Indian say the same.[2]

In some of the interviews we conducted they mentioned racism they had faced from their own family members, whether that be their birth parents, step-parents, in-laws or extended family. This isn't limited to those with white family members. Some people we spoke to felt prejudice from their non-white side of the family, especially around the narrative of, 'You're not black enough or Asian enough', and so on. Also, having a family member who is BIPOC doesn't stop prejudices that occur in different communities, i.e. anti-Asian and anti-Black sentiments. Some knew from early on that their family members' language and views were racist and others didn't recognise it until much later. The impact of both is devastating. For some of you who are mixed race with white family members, you may well have encountered racist attitudes and comments. While they may 'accept you' because you are a relative, there will be problematic behaviour or ignorance around how racism operates. They might say things like, 'I've got no issue with coloured people,' and believe that because their grandchild/ nephew/daughter-in-law etc. isn't racialised as white they surely cannot be racist. They might also cite having a relative who is non-white as a shield against anyone who accuses them of being racist.

The truth is, just as it's possible for a man to have a wife and be sexist, it's possible for a white person to have a non-white person in their family, and still be a racist. Having mixed-race children or being in a mixed-race relationship does not give you a free pass. In fact, you should be taking full responsibility for your learning about how systemic racism and oppressive structures work to ensure that you do not inflict harm or add further trauma to those people you love. It's certainly not as if the literature and resources aren't available.

Racism within the family is not always overt and doesn't always manifest in the form of microaggressions. For many BIPOC people who live with or visit their white family members, this can also arise in the objects that are found in the family home. These could be items you may have been wary of, or there might have been something that did not sit right with you during your childhood, but only now that you're older do you realise how problematic those things are. Golliwogs, memorabilia with racist images, paintings or racist ornaments around the home, are all examples of these.

Another way racism can manifest in these settings can include race never being mentioned or being ignored, and there being nothing in the home that represents you or other parts of your identity. You may not have any knowledge of, or references to, your heritage; you may have been referred to as 'white' by your parents, as well as other scenarios like having no Black or brown dolls to play with or books with anyone like you reflected in them.

On 8 March 2021 Kemah Bob, comedian and writer put out the tweet: 'I don't think the racism mixed race kids face from their own families is discussed enough.' Hundreds replied to the tweet with stories of their own experiences growing up in racist households:[3]

Someone on my white side knitted me a gollywog and brought it to the hospital when I was born.

I'm mixed race and my sister is also (both adopted). One of my aunts seemed aghast at the fact that my parents were going to actually tell people my sister was half-Pakistani and half-Greek. Aunt suggested saying she was Spanish or 'Mediterranean' to make it more acceptable.

When I was younger, and I used to visit my mum's side they were so ashamed to have a half-black grandchild they kept us locked in a room and we weren't allowed to go out for guests to see us. From as young as 3 they kept telling my mum to bleach my skin. We never spoke to them again.

I remember my (white) dad took me to visit some of his family. His aunt took him aside and told him not quietly to never bring his ch*nk children ever again. I think about that a lot.

~~~

Speaking to your family about race

Following the murder of George Floyd in May 2020, many people found themselves talking about race in an unprecedented way. For some, this meant talking about racism within their family and friendship groups for the first time. Undoubtedly, it would have been painful. For others, it may have been a relief. Perhaps it felt like the elephant in the room had finally been tackled. Some families will still be navigating the fallout. One thing is for sure, many of these conversations would have been met with the realisation of *'Oh God, my family is racist, what do I do now?'*

For many mixed-race people growing up in a household where it's only you that looks like you, these conversations are more likely to be complex and hard to navigate. Having to speak about anything when you are not sure how the other people will respond can induce anxiety and can often lead to avoidance. To have to speak to your own family – people you love and care for – about your identity and lived experience, and to be met with gaslighting and white fragility, is a traumatic experience. These discussions can become uncomfortable, emotional and at times, unsafe. In our interviews, many people shared how, when they brought up racism or challenged white family members, they were met with defensive attitudes, white tears and deflection. The experience of having to have a conversation about how you feel, being in triggering situations and having to relay experiences which have upset you as a mixed-race person, juxtaposed with your family members responding with emotive reactions (thus making you feel guilty and needing to comfort them) once again results in your feelings being pushed to the side and places them in the position of the victim. As well as you being the one who is *actually* being victimised this also (wrongly) positions you in the place of the aggressor, which is harmful.

Michelle (she/her) is a mother and creator from the north of England. She identifies as a Black mixed-race woman (white English, Black Jamaican and Chinese). Michelle is married to T J, her husband, who is also of mixed heritage (Bajan and Nigerian) and they share three children. She shares with us some of her experiences of racism within her own family.

Naomi and Natalie: What was it like growing up as a mixed-race woman in your family?

Michelle: Difficult on so many levels. I actually didn't fully awaken to how difficult [it was] until last year and the killing of George Floyd. I grew up in the white northern docking city of Salford, plagued with poverty and a lack of opportunities. The threat of anyone different was always met with resistance, especially with the added lack of education or experience; these elements are true of many of my family members too. Don't get me wrong, I was very much loved, but my Blackness wasn't. I also was the eldest, with four younger siblings. The racism directed sometimes was disguised behind the fact my mum (white) and dad (Black) had a very difficult and toxic

131

relationship after they separated. My dad and his Blackness were often an opportunity for people to be racist [hiding behind the pretence that it was due to them not liking the situation with him and my mum].

I was around stories of my mum being told by her stepfather she was 'no good' and 'that's why she's with a Black man' as 'no respectful white man would have her'. All those old chestnuts. I have the most wonderful Black mixed-race stepdad who was married to my mum from when I was a toddler. I would hear family members say, 'Oh, isn't Wayne lovely for a Black man?' As I got older, I constantly felt it was a battle and was told I was on my soap box as I navigated through a sea of flippant racist language and behaviour, from my nickname being 'Choco' to constantly having to have very heated discussions with my beloved nana, our matriarch, about her racist views.

Naomi and Natalie: Have you ever experienced racism within your own family?

Michelle: Plenty of times. I remember in the eighties, my mum, dad and us kids not being invited to a big family wedding due to the fact my mum was married to a Black man. Apparently, the bride's brother had been beaten up by some Black youths and that was the reason they didn't want my Black dad and his children in attendance. My great-grandma at the time said she wouldn't attend unless we were all invited, which triggered them to invite us. They put us in the cheap seats near the swinging kitchen doors. My mum wasn't aware at the time and now hates the fact we went. There was also constant language microaggressions. My brother has lighter skin, and my nana constantly would say he would pass for white.

Naomi and Natalie: What advice would you give to mixed-race people who are dealing with racism in their family? How can they look after themselves?

Michelle: I would say to always feel confident in calling it out, regardless. I do hope that some people can change with education and understanding. I would constantly say to family, 'How would you feel if someone spoke that way about me?'

Don't be afraid to cut people out of your life. It's already hard enough carrying the weight of the struggles you face being mixed in a world that doesn't love and embrace you. Any toxic or damaging relationship – get rid!

Kayleigh (she/her) works in finance, and grew up in Worthing. She lived in south London for a while (during her teens) and has now moved back to Worthing. She identifies as mixed race and is of Black African and white British heritage.

Naomi and Natalie: Can you tell us a bit about your upbringing?

Kayleigh: My birth father is from Tanzania and my mum is white British. That said, he wasn't around, so I grew up with my stepdad who is Jamaican. Culturally, growing up was very much with a Caribbean background as opposed to the African side. I grew up kind of all over the place – down on the south coast near Brighton, then a stint in south London, and a little bit of time in Kenya. Now, I work in and live back by the coast.

Naomi and Natalie: Can you recall an incident of racism in your own family?

133

Kayleigh: My uncle posted something on Facebook around Anthony Joshua and the Black Lives Matter movement, basically being like, 'I'm bored of this conversation, blah, blah, blah.' And he rang up my mum and said, 'Kayleigh's blocked me on Facebook.' I said, 'I don't care who he is. He could be the Queen; I don't care, I am not putting up with it. I will call you out.' That comes from my mum giving me the space to do that and being the person that's like, no, this isn't acceptable; stand up for yourself. Growing up in that environment where I could do that. There are some people that I've met who are like, 'actually, no, I haven't been able to do that. Actually, I've felt trapped in that space. And it's not something I can do.'

You have probably read *Why I'm No Longer Talking to White People About Race* and in there, you're being told to protect and prepare for what it's going to be like going into the world as a Black person where things are stacked against you. If you're mixed and surrounded by predominantly white family, you don't get that, right? You kind of go out on your own and then you're like, 'Oh, wow, this is interesting. This is new.' This is something I now have to experience and navigate often without the kind of coaching and help that some would have at home. If you're Black and have a Black family, you are more equipped. You just don't have that coming from the other side. My mum is brilliant, but she's always put her hands up and said, 'I don't know what that feels like.' She's always been very open and honest about that. But it definitely means there's something missing there.

The impact of having racist family members can be considerable and difficult to navigate, from avoiding family gatherings to feelings of self-hatred. It is already a traumatic and exhausting experience, having to challenge and navigate racism in your daily life, without then having to do it with your own family members. This is more than having different views on what you should have for dinner that evening, it's not a 'let's agree to disagree' moment. It's deeper because this is your lived experience and linked to your identity.

Reasons why it's difficult to speak out:

1. Fear of causing upset.
2. Feeling there is no one to back you up.
3. Not wanting to ruin a family gathering.
4. Fear of being gaslighted, or called 'over-sensitive'.

Recent events in the world may well have opened up thoughts and feelings that you haven't processed before. It's important you don't go through this on your own. There are lots of guides out there on how to talk to people about racism, but very few of them acknowledge that it's very different if you are doing it as a mixed-race person within your own family. The additional trauma and sense of betrayal in having to speak on the matter to people you feel should be advocating for you is incredibly painful, but there are ways you can protect yourself and speaking honestly with those you love can lead to healing, even if it's just for you. You do not have to tolerate racism from people because they are your family members. By setting clear boundaries, you are standing up for yourself; never let anyone convince you otherwise. If you have grown up with a racist family member, you may benefit from counselling and professional support.

Boundaries can look like:

1. Making the decision to stop allowing someone access to you for your own mental wellbeing. Constantly having to debate and defend your own humanity with a family member is not healthy and therefore, you may have no choice but to end the relationship or, at the very least, limit your interactions.
2. You may decide that while you cannot or do not want to end the relationship, you no longer want to enter into discussions about race with that person. You may decide to create boundaries around what you will and won't speak about in order to protect yourself.
3. Writing a letter to communicate how you feel and what you would like to see going forward in the relationship. You may have never been able to explain to this person how you really feel and writing down your thoughts can be a good place to start, even if it ends up just being for you.
4. Accepting it's not your job to educate your whole family, especially if you are in a predominantly white family as a mixed-race person.
5. Recognising that you do not have to apologise for challenging racism.
6. Not visiting family members or attending social gatherings without a friend or partner with you – someone you trust and who understands the situation.

It is not only overt racism that exists in families. When you are different in skin colour to the majority of your family, there will always be a lack of understanding around your experience, and we're not only just talking about the white side of families. There are times when perhaps you feel you are not enough for either part of your family or there are things that you are unable to speak about because it will be met with a lack of understanding. Like the rest of us, your parents and family will not be immune from conscious and unconscious bias. There will be things you want to talk about, which they will never fully grasp and there will be times when they respond in a really unhelpful way. That's why it's important to have somebody you can speak to who has a shared lived experience and who you are able to speak honestly with. Look for the allies within your family or friendship groups; be honest with them about how you feel.

Phrases to help you construct your boundaries with family:

1. 'I want to make it clear that I love you, but when we are in the same space together, I have the right to not listen to offensive comments. If you love and respect me, I will ask you not to say ____/these things.'
2. 'We all have prejudices, even me. Just because you have a ____ friend, colleague, partner, family member does not make you immune to being racist.'
3. 'I would like to talk to you more about this, but now is not the right time. Could we stop this conversation and pick it up later?'
4. 'I have heard people saying that, but I've been watching/ reading/listening to X. If you want to understand where I'm coming from, maybe you could do the same?'
5. 'If we are going to spend time together going forward, I would ask that you refrain from doing/saying this ____.'
6. 'I am comfortable in talking about ____, but I am not going to talk about this with you if you shout or raise your voice.'

Reflections:

1. Have you given yourself the time and space to reflect on the dynamics within your family and how they respond to race?
2. Have you been trying to single-handedly educate your family members on different issues?
3. How has this impacted you?
4. Do you need to put some boundaries in place with your family members?
5. What boundaries do you need to put in place to ensure a healthier relationship with your family?
6. Are there toxic relationships that need to be addressed?
7. How are you healing from traumatic experiences with your family?
8. What can you put in place to begin the healing process?

Chapter 7

'I didn't think they were your type':

On interracial relationships

~~~

Naomi: I am married to a white man who is of English and Irish heritage. Our first date was at a run-down Bohemian-style bar by the sea, which I loved (and which I later found out he hated, but pretended to like in a bid to impress me). On the date, I was pretty vocal about the political party I voted for in order to gauge whether we were aligned in how we felt. It was at the height of UKIP's popularity in our hometown (an independent party which had strong anti-EU and anti-immigration policies and lots of racist members). For me, if he signified any preference to a party like that it would have been game over and saved me from any further wasted dates. He didn't say anything that set off alarm bells and despite later telling me he actually didn't like the bar we had gone to, we got married in 2013. Over our ten-year relationship things have come up along the way that have demonstrated his naivety to how racism operates. Thankfully, we have always been able to talk things through, but there are times when he himself will admit he has become defensive. In June 2020 we were watching a news report which featured Patrick Hutchinson, the personal trainer and author of *Everyone Versus Racism*, who rose to prominence after he was photographed carrying an injured white counter-protestor to safety in a BLM march.

This was a deeply difficult time in our household. We were also in the midst of a lockdown, attempting to home-school two small children while also working as teachers. There was fierce criticism of the BLM movement from the government, in the media and even from some people we knew. I didn't have to explain it to my husband; he was in full support and that summer we'd marched together with our children and 4,000 others in our hometown. He was also reading Layla

F. Saad's *Me and White Supremacy*,[1] after our ongoing discussions about learning more on the subject. When Hutchinson started to speak in the TV interview, the words 'He's really well spoken' fell out of my husband's mouth. I turned and looked at him. He could tell by my face I wasn't happy.

'What do you mean?' I asked.
'He's really well spoken,' he repeated.
'Would you have said that if he was white?'
'Oh, don't try and make it into something,' he said.

I was so angry. The rage inside me boiled up. Not only did I have to listen to debates about whether racism was as bad as people were saying and face the vitriol on social media, but I was also now getting defensive responses from my husband. I felt alone, betrayed and tearful. The next day, we sat down, and I explained why what he said was problematic and how his response had been even worse. It was frustrating having to explain to my husband, the person I am closest to, that our unconscious bias will show up, even with the best intentions. We are in a place where we can talk things out together, but we also have to accept this won't be the last time issues like this will arise. Any relationship requires space to be able to listen to each other. There is no way we would survive if we didn't.

While mixed-race relationships are now on the rise in both the UK and US they are not a new phenomenon although even in contemporary times they have not always been accepted by society, or even legal. In South Africa under apartheid laws passed in 1949, marriages between white people and anyone deemed to be 'non-white' were illegal.[2] Although there were no formal laws in the UK forbidding interracial relationships there was plenty of opposition some of which was rooted in advocacy of eugenics. In 1934 Marie Stopes, author, women's rights campaigner, and eugenicist publicly called for the sterilisation of 'half-castes'.[3] During 1950s America, interracial relationships were outlawed in thirty-one states, only becoming legal under the ruling of the Supreme Court in the Loving vs Virginia case, in 1967. As a result, the 12th of June is now recognised as National Loving Day in the United States, named after Mildred Loving, a woman who identified as Indian-Rappahannock, but was reported to be of Cherokee, Portuguese and African American ancestry, and her husband Richard P. Loving, a white American, who were jailed in 1958 on charges of unlawful cohabitation. Although the couple were married in Washington D.C., they returned to their hometown in Virginia where it was illegal to be in an interracial marriage even if it had taken place out of state. After being found guilty, they were given the option to avoid their jail term if they left Virginia. As such, they decided to return to the District of Columbia. The couple wrote a letter to the then United States Attorney General, Robert F. Kennedy and the case eventually made its way to the Supreme Court, who ruled that 'The freedom to marry, or not marry, a person of another race resides with the individual, and cannot be infringed by the state.'[4]

In the United States, there has been a steady rise in interracial marriage. As of 2016, 10.2 per cent of married people living together were in an interracial relationship (up from 7.4 per cent in 2012). In the UK, according to the 2011 census, one in ten people (2.3 million) said they were in an interracial relationship (an increase of 7 per cent from 2001). White British people were least likely to be in mixed-race relationships, followed by Bangladeshi, Pakistani and Indian ethnic groups. The biggest difference between the sexes was found within the Chinese community, where women were almost twice as likely (39 per cent) to be in an interracial relationship as men.[5]

Interracial relationships can open us up to new cultures, experiences and a whole new family. I fondly remember how much my Black

Jamaican grandmother loved my white British mum. If it wasn't
for my parents' interracial relationship, they never would have
crossed paths. She loved her like her own daughter – yes, they'd
clash over cooking or how to do my hair – but when we would visit
her in Jamaica, she'd cry when she left. It was genuine love. Of
course, there can be many challenges and causes of contention.
While your partner may be open and understanding, there is the
possibility that their family may not be. There are also situations in
which family members are opposed to interracial relationships or
overtly racist.

**Our mum, Penelope, reflects on when she first met our dad, George, in
the seventies:**

Naomi and Natalie: Can you tell us about when you first met Dad and
what it was like being in an interracial relationship in a white-majority
town?

Mum: I first met your dad in 1975. He was one of the few Black people
in the area. To be honest, I didn't appreciate people's attitudes . . . [they
were] quite a shock to me. It started probably with somebody at work.
Your dad used to come in and see me in the evening during my shift
and sit with me. One night my work colleague saw him and said to me,
'Is that your boyfriend?'

I said, 'Yes,' and she replied, 'Oh yeah, I've got another friend who
goes out with Black men.' I said, 'Well, I don't "go out with Black men",
I just go out with him.'

I think I became aware that our dating attracted quite a lot of attention.
Not necessarily negative, but you felt very conspicuous. For example,
when we went to a nightclub or we were walking, I was conscious that

people looked, it was a really odd feeling. I came to realise actually that there was a lot more reaction from people than I anticipated.

Your dad was also well known in the sports circles [for] playing football. I became very aware of the racism he experienced in football on the pitch, which was just largely ignored. I don't think people necessarily condoned it, but nothing was challenged. We went to a party one night with this group of football friends and this guy told a very blatant racist joke. By that time, I think I was a little bit more questioning. I said to him, 'Why are you telling racist jokes?' He went, 'Oh, it's all right, George don't mind; he is my mate.' Your dad didn't really want me to go on, so I shut up in the end.

Naomi and Natalie: When you met Dad, did you ever think about what going into an interracial relationship would be like?

Mum: Nope, I was naive to be honest. It was difficult because I didn't want to make him feel more uncomfortable by challenging things, so it was a hard dynamic. I do remember one particular incident, right when I first started going out with him. When we were walking down the road, it was quite common practice for your dad to say hi to another Black person if he saw them. Even if he didn't know them, it was a shared experience. On this one occasion, a couple of guys drove past in the car and shouted at him and he waved at them and then they shouted racial abuse at him. It was awful. I didn't know what to say, I was shocked.

Naomi and Natalie: What was your experience and the prejudice that you received dating a black man or was it aimed more towards Dad?

Mum: It was more towards him. I was aware there was some prejudice. I can't recall anybody overtly saying anything to me. I do remember a couple of inappropriate jokes about Black men, comments rooted in fetishisation. It was never said to me in a vicious way. I was just uncomfortable; that was probably my experience more than anything.

Naomi and Natalie: What about culturally? Your two worlds coming together?

Mum: There were obviously cultural differences. I used to go and visit his Jamaican family in Nottingham, and it was a very different family culture. Good things, like food, etc . . .

I used to try my hand at rice and peas and things like that, which I know he appreciated, though he might have laughed sometimes at my cooking. When I had you girls, I learned that Black hair is a huge cultural thing, and it needs care. When I first met your dad, he had an Afro, but then we went through the fashion of the wet-look perm. He had a lot of products for that, and we used to laugh about it, really, but the product would get all over the pillows, in my hair, on the back of chairs! Then he used to wear a plastic cap to keep the gel in. So, there was that part of it, which I sort of tried to get. Every now and then he would revert to Patois particularly with his family which I didn't really understand. Music was also a huge thing. I learned a lot about music through your dad that I didn't know about before, such as Motown, soul and reggae. I think probably more when you girls were born, the cultural aspects become more prominent, including approaches to parenting.

Naomi and Natalie: How was the relationship from within the family, especially both of your parents?

Mum: Oh, that was interesting. His mother really liked me. She would come and stay for long periods of time, and I think like with any in-laws, it had its moments. I remember one time she came to visit from America, and she would bring gifts from the big American outlet stores. She was a real bargain hunter which I loved. She also used to bring over food, and she brought over a Christmas cake with all the rum, and I would ice it and we would have that for dessert. She also used to bring a cooked turkey in a shopping bag on the plane, so you can imagine it sweated quite a bit before it got here! I was always a bit nervous of this turkey, but in Jamaican culture, nothing goes to waste. We were expected to eat this whole turkey to the bone and once it had been hanging around for a week, I was really not keen on eating the turkey. I know she used to get annoyed about that, and waste. In regard to my parents, they seemed quite accepting on the outside, but clearly, they weren't because when I got engaged to your dad and he wanted to ask my father for permission, my father said to him, 'I like you, George but I don't approve of mixed marriages because it's not fair to children,' which was a pretty horrendous thing to say. I'll be honest; I never, ever spoke to my dad about it. It was so hard because they loved your dad, and we would spend Christmas with them. Your dad used to really like going to my parents' home, he was very well liked by everyone. We still got engaged and we had an engagement party, but I couldn't entertain why my father said what he said. I know I should have said something, but it was hard and because I had made up my mind that I was marrying your dad, I didn't feel that having that conversation would make any difference.

Here are some of the challenges that show up when it comes to interracial dating, partnerships and marriage:

1. Fear about what the other person might say when it comes to you and your family's racial heritage.
2. Lack of understanding about your lived experience.
3. Gaslighting phrases – such as 'Don't be so sensitive', or 'They didn't mean it that way' – when you explain a situation or issue that has occurred.

4. Microaggressions, such as 'You're pretty for a _____'; 'Is that your real hair?'; 'Where are you really from?'; 'You don't look like you are _____'.

5. Concern about meeting each other's families.

6. Lack of acceptance from one or both sides of the family.

7. Differences in how you approach decisions based on your cultural heritage.

8. Tension due to conflicting values.

9. Assumptions based on how the other person is racialised.

10. Racist family members and how to deal with them.

11. Lack of willingness to address conscious and unconscious bias (for example, the white partner thinking they get a free pass because they are in an interracial relationship).

12. Fetishisation – making someone an object of desire because of an aspect of their identity.

Sushmita (she/her) is in her early thirties and was born and raised in Mumbai, India. She met her husband when she came to study in the UK. He is white British. They live in Kent with their three children.

Sushmita: Because it took me ages to recognise and understand racism, I had to point it out to my husband. Certain things he did or said, that we laughed at in the past, are no longer allowed. He could be teasing me about my accent. I questioned that for a long time, like, is it OK for him to do that? When I actually did tell him, he got really upset because of this idea that 'I have mixed-race kids and I have you, I'm not racist.' I wasn't saying 'you're racist'. What I was trying to say was that certain things were unacceptable. Yes, I put up with it in the past and I wouldn't even say anything before, I probably participated in it quite happily. But since becoming more aware and more sensitive to these things, I was finding it difficult.

Michael spoke to us about his experience of being in an interracial marriage with Hannah.

Naomi and Natalie: When it comes to your marriage, are there any things that have been difficult or things you have found that have helped you?

Michael: Hannah and I were friends before we entered into a relationship. I think that helped how we bonded. We didn't come together because of our identity or our backgrounds. It was because we just really liked each other and we gave each other different experiences. That's something I would definitely say is a positive.

I think Hannah has learned a great deal since she's had the children, in terms of her understanding as an educator and learning what is said and what attitudes are formed in the classroom from teacher to pupil. But that's something that we definitely talk about.

I engage in a fostering agency as well, so I really have a good understanding of children coming into the care system which leads into education, so we talk a great deal about experiences of looked-after children, of which the majority are from minority ethnic backgrounds. We have a love of learning and working together and talking about different things. Because of certain movements that have happened in the last four years (we've been together fifteen years) it's been eleven years of her and other people just not necessarily seeing it. It has been a massive confidence boost for me for Hannah to say things such as 'Oh, that person didn't even acknowledge you in that queue today,' or 'That was a bit of a strange way to react when you're just trying to ask somebody something in a restaurant,' or whatever it may be. It's just slowly but surely. I think there's a lot of awakening happening with people that don't go through some of these experiences that perhaps you and I have.

Sandra* (she/her) is a midwife based in Norwich in the UK. She identifies as Black Caribbean (her father is British and Jamaican, her mother was born in Jamaica and moved to the UK when she was fourteen years old). She is married to her husband who is white Spanish. Both their families are Muslim converts. They have one daughter together who is three years old.

Naomi and Natalie: What were some of the challenges you faced as a mixed-race couple?

Sandra: One of the biggest challenges was meeting each other's families. I feel like in a lot of Black households where both parents are Black and the children are Black, the humour and the family dynamics are often very different. The hierarchical aspect of the family is very different to a lot of white English families or white families generally. I think when meeting, parents were fine, but like extended family or older grandparents or whatever was a bit more complicated. Where my husband lived in Spain, the Black people that a lot of them saw, were migrants or people who were like selling stuff on the side of the road. Black people weren't among them in their family. So when I came along, it was like, 'Oh, hello.' My husband's grandma would be like, 'La Negrita' (meaning 'the little Black one'). Actually, my husband's cousin met my brother at our wedding, and they ended up getting married three years later. His grandma said, 'I never expected a Black person to be in my family.'

Isaac (he/him) and Emma (she/her) are married with one child. Isaac is in his early thirties, is Black British and of Ghanaian heritage. Emma is in her late twenties and is white British. They live in London.

Naomi and Natalie: In terms of your relationship, how did you navigate bringing two cultures together?

Isaac: Let's just say we had to do some acclimatising. I was brought up a certain way and being Ghanaian influenced that, and Emma being English influenced her upbringing. We had our separate ways, and the challenge was finding a new way together that respected where we were both coming from. In my family we call all the elders uncle and auntie as a sign of respect. That was something I felt was important and wanted me and my new family to do, so I communicated that.

Emma: Yeah, and I guess for me there were things that I did when I was growing up that I really valued, like having dinner around the table with my family every night. Isaac said he didn't really do that growing up. I communicated that it is something I'd like to keep doing and now we do it too. When I look at the times we clashed, it was mainly because we didn't communicate in the best way, but whenever you understand why something is important to someone, it becomes quite easy to respect it.

Isaac: Obviously, it's not always clear-cut, but you just have to try and find a middle ground. It's part of being in an interracial relationship. I think the goal is to be empathetic and understanding without losing who you are at your core. Whenever we feel like we might be losing who we are, that's when we feel the pressure on us as a couple.

Natalie: 'Do you have a type?' is one of the main questions I think we all get asked when on the dating scene. For me, I feel as though this question is much more layered, maybe I am thinking too much into it, but there are times when I felt what people were actually asking was, 'Do you prefer Black or white guys?' Looking at my dating history I have dated white men, Asian men and Black men, but when I was using the dating app Hinge in 2019, I noticed I was only swiping for Black men.

Growing up, I soon found out that white men were never interested in me. I never had a boyfriend at school. All my friends were dating, and I was the only one who wasn't. It seemed to me that skinny, white, blonde girls were the boys' preferred type at school – and I never fitted that mould, no matter how hard I tried.

My partner is Jamaican. I remember our first phone call, when I asked him about his heritage. He told me that both his parents were first-generation Jamaicans. On our first date he bought me a book, it was titled, *How to Love a Jamaican* by Alexia Arthurs, a collection of short stories about Jamaican migrants and their families. It was a beautiful gesture and one I will never forget. The truth was I was hesitant about dating a Jamaican man. It's hard to admit because now I feel ashamed of having thought in this way. There were stereotypes around Jamaican men that I had internalised, that I had reinforced after seeing some of these stereotypes manifest in my own family setting. Because of these instances, I wanted to stay far away from Jamaican men. As we have learned by now, we all have biases, and this was definitely one of mine.

In 2021 Inner Circle in collaboration with Tineka Smith and Alex Court, authors of *Mixed Up* published the 'Mixed Up in Love' report. They surveyed over 1,000 UK adults actively dating. Forty-nine per cent of them stated that they feared backlash or criticism from those closest to them for dating interracially. When it came to dating apps, 44 per cent felt self-conscious about their race or ethnic background and 3 in 10 respondents said they experienced racial microaggressions when using them.[6]

As an interracial couple, my husband and I were surprised about the discrimination we've faced over the years which led us to write about our experiences in the book MIXED UP: Confessions of an Interracial Couple. *There aren't many spaces that highlight the racial aggressions mixed-race couples face from strangers, friends and family as well as racial struggles that can happen within those relationships. This lack of acknowledgement in the public space surrounding racism – specifically towards mixed-race couples – makes it easy for others to brush these problems aside. I felt vindicated when 'The Mixed Up in Love' report was released because it showed that my husband and I weren't alone in our experiences and feelings, and that many people are nervous about dating outside their race because of potential backlash. It's really a shame and shows racially we still have a long way to go as a society. The UK has serious racial issues but will never progress as long as people continue to deny there's a problem to begin with.*

Tineka Smith

The survey also found that over a third of respondents had experienced racial fetishisation. In a recent study with dating app Bumble, the report surveyed 1,004 adults in the UK which found that the group most likely to experience fetishisation were mixed-race men and women followed by Asian and Black women. The survey revealed that 53 per cent of people in the study did not have a clear understanding of what fetishisation is.[7] Fetishisation occurs when someone is made an object of sexual desire based on a part of their identity, although it can often be disguised by someone expressing a 'preference'. From the hyper-masculinisation of Black men to the 'submissive but highly sexualised' trope projected on Asian women, racialised people are certainly familiar with these racist tropes. In dating, fetishisation can sound like 'You're so exotic', 'Latin women are so hot', 'Once you go Black, you never go back'. It serves as another way to dehumanise People of Colour and, of course, makes navigating relationships for BIPOC far more difficult.

We spoke again to Kayleigh about her experience of dating.

Naomi and Natalie: Do you mind if we ask you a bit about dating? Because that's actually something we haven't talked about with a lot of people.

Kayleigh: I definitely feel like it went through phases. Like it was trends of who everyone wanted to be with. There was that time, maybe around 2013–2014, when [pop star] Rihanna went red. All the boys were obsessed with Rihanna. Everyone dyed their hair red. But I wondered were the boys actually attracted to me or was it the trendy thing to be attracted' to right now? I went to school with predominantly white girls and the boys' school opposite was nearly all white boys. It was expected that I would fancy the Black guy. Growing up in a predominantly white area, I would say I was more attracted to white guys because that was who I'd been around. I got with my ex (a white man) when I was seventeen. All his exes before had been very, very slim blonde girls, so when we got together, I had a lot of doubts. I worried, *Is he attracted to me? Is this a weird experiment?* We were together for four years and the whole time I never, ever felt I was quite what he wanted. I do feel like with some white men, I've definitely been fetishised. I went on an awful date and he literally said to me something along the lines of basically, 'You're really pretty and I like that you don't have the "Black girl attitude".' My face obviously dropped, and he was like, 'I don't mean it like that, it's a good thing.' I had just started working in London and I'd just turned twenty-one. I remember I didn't date for months after that. I've definitely had the experience of feeling fetishised on one end of the spectrum with some white men, but similarly with Black men too. A lot of it comes from media culture, rap videos and being fed ideas that you should want a light-skinned girl, it's all like, 'I want to date the "pretty lighty".'

~

Important things to remember in an interracial relationship:

1. Get comfortable with difficult conversations. Do not avoid talking about race. It may be uncomfortable but staying silent won't solve anything and will also lead to far more difficult issues further down the road. Just like any relationship, being honest and open is essential.

2. Be prepared that your relationship may be met with resistance and pushback from others. For example, you may live in a diverse or metropolitan area but when you travel elsewhere, others may not be accepting of you or your partner.

3. Discuss how you would like the other person to respond when you know you are coming up against difficult situations. For example, a family gathering with a racist relative. It's important you work as a team.

4. In a new relationship, ask questions that acknowledge racism is not something that can be brushed under the carpet.

5. Talk with your partner about their dating history and openly ask questions you wish to know more about.

6. If your partner is new to talking about racism, do not expect them to become an expert overnight. The important thing is they are committed to listening, growing and changing in the areas they need to. If you experience gaslighting behaviour from your partner, or they try to engage you in debate on your lived experience, you need to question if you are in a safe and healthy relationship.

7. Do not make assumptions about your partner because of their race. Remember racial groups are not a monolith.

8. Keep in mind we are all guilty of stereotyping and hold our own implicit biases.

9. Make connections with other people who can support you. There will be times when you may need advice from an

interracial couple who have been through the things you have, or even seek counselling. There is no shame in getting help and it's important to normalise being honest about struggles.

10. You may feel an increased sense of wanting to assert your heritage and culture. It's natural to want to ensure your identity is not erased when you share your life with someone who is different to you. Talk about what's important to you or other ways in which you feel you are preserving, recognising and being connected to your culture and heritage.

Chapter 8

'I've always wanted a mixed-race baby':

On raising mixed-race children

~

Naomi: There are many wonderful things about being part of a multiracial family and raising mixed-race children. If you are the parent or caregiver to a mixed-race child, there will also be many things to consider and be mindful of, some of which you may have never thought about. We hope that this chapter will help you to feel more confident, but above all, ensure the children in your care learn to love and grow in their identity as opposed to feeling confused or like an outsider in their own family. Of course, being mixed race will not be their only identity and it's important to acknowledge that this will be fluid and open to change, but the most important thing is creating a space in which your children can talk to you without fear or worry of rejection. You may not understand their lived experience, but you can offer an environment of love and safety. If you have older children or teenagers and have not approached these issues yet, it is not too late and it is also important to admit that you may not have realised some of these things until now, but you are open to learning and growing. If we want our children to grow up comfortable exploring their identity, we need to be intentional about not repeating mistakes from the past.

Our mum, Penelope, explains how things have changed from her perspective when she brought us up during the eighties and nineties.

Naomi and Natalie: Thinking about when you were raising us to what you see now do you think there are many differences? Is there more support for raising mixed-race children?

Mum: There were times when I had to make it up as I went along and there were other times where I did try and read literature. I read a lot of books through work because I was a social worker. In the early days, a lot of literature was very negative. It spoke about attitudes towards mixed-race relationships and marriages, and I read some really horrible stuff, particularly around the very early language used towards mixed-heritage people. I think the language has changed to a degree. It still has its limitations, but we have come a long way from 'half-caste', 'coloured', 'mixed blood'. I still don't love 'mixed race'; I use dual heritage, but I know it's up to you how you identify and what you want to say. A lot of what I used to read was all very much based on historical theories and ideas of 'inferior biological factors and intelligence'; it was awful. It spoke about how the more you mix, the more it will ruin everything. It's shocking when you look back. I would find that very uncomfortable reading now, as I did then. In the early days a lot of the research I would do with social work was around the negative impact on the child's identity, and there was a lot of writing at one time about not placing Black and brown children with white families because they didn't have the skills to bring them up and the child would have a damaged identity. That felt uncomfortable as well because I raised you and I know you had influence from your father and his family, but ultimately, this research was saying that you would have poor identity and self-esteem, which wasn't a very pleasant thing. Things changed a bit and I think it swung more to saying as long as people have the right skills, then it doesn't have to be negative, which I think can be true. But going back to your question, I didn't have the right resources. This book is the book I wish I had.

The fetishisation of mixed-race children

How many times have you heard someone say phrases like 'I want mixed-race babies; they are so cute,' or 'Mixed-race kids are the best of both worlds'? Children under the age of sixteen account for 47 per cent of the mixed-race population in the UK.[1] After children racialised as white, mixed-race children are the most represented group in the care system accounting for 10% of the 80,000 looked after children in the UK.[2] At the same time, there is a worrying trend of social media accounts dedicated to mixed-race children with hashtags such as #mixedbabies, #perfectlyblended and #swirl. Of course, there's nothing wrong with sharing pictures of your family or celebrating your interracial relationships, but we must address the issues around fetishisation of mixed-race children and often the notion that light-skinned mixed-race children with Eurocentric features are the ideal, offering something 'exotic' or 'interesting'. The objectification of mixed-race children is very real and also presents an unrealistic and idealistic view of what it can be like to grow up as a multiracial person.

Issues with fetishisation:

- Focusing purely on the exterior beauty of children is damaging.
- It perpetuates colourism and upholds anti-Blackness.
- It neglects to acknowledge the complexities there can be of growing up mixed race and projects a perfect veneer, which some people will find it hard to live up to.
- It turns mixed-race children into a 'trend' and fails to acknowledge them as full individuals.
- It dehumanises mixed-race children and feeds into racist tropes such as 'exoticism'.

Another issue that arises when people are raising mixed-race children is that they can neglect to address or even acknowledge their own racism or prejudice. Being in a multiracial relationship doesn't make you immune from racism; conversely, having children doesn't make you exempt from upholding racist ideology. Failure to acknowledge your conscious or unconscious bias is harmful and will certainly impact negatively on your children. And this doesn't only apply to white parents.

161

The assumption that your child is going to be more secure in their mixed-race identity because the main caregiver is a Person of Colour is naive. Of course, there are so many layers to this. If we had been raised by a Black mother of Jamaican heritage, or we had spent more of our childhood with our father, then perhaps we would have initially had more connection to our heritage and culture. However, there are many variables which will influence your experience, from the area where you grew up, the school you attended and who you spend time with. If you are growing up as a mixed-race person in a white-majority area your experience is going to be dramatically different to that of someone in a more multicultural environment. For monoracial parents, telling your mixed-race children how to identify is problematic, despite how you perceive them. Identity is something that as an individual, we shape ourselves. While we may have similar experiences to white, Black, Asian or other racialised groups, we sometimes have our own experience – the mixed-race experience.

There is also the reality that there are parents of mixed-race children who still think that anti-racism doesn't apply to them. That somehow by having children with someone who isn't white they have 'proven' themselves or are somehow immune to perpetuating white supremacy. We're not always referring to parents displaying overt racism, although unfortunately this does still happen. Sometimes it is the small things, things we may not even consider that can have an impact.

My husband and I have two young children who are of mixed heritage. One of our boys has very tight curly hair and he likes to fiddle with the curls to the point that some of them started to look like locs. I suggested that we ask him if he wanted locs and my husband replied, 'No, I don't like them. They look messy.' I was really angry. Someone at work had made a similar comment to me a few weeks previously when talking about locs and I was

*annoyed with myself that I hadn't challenged it. I told him that he
was viewing it through a white lens and that I didn't want our sons
to have the message that there was anything wrong with having
locs and that he was so conditioned to what he thought 'good hair'
was, it was going to influence our children.*

Sharron*

Not interrogating your biases and prejudicial thoughts is dangerous.
Not only because you are not being honest with yourself, but because
of the impact this could have on your children. Our systems and
structures have been set up to benefit those closest to 'whiteness'. We
are all capable of upholding racist ideology. Being white and having
children who are mixed race does not mean you cannot be racist. It's
also not something you can change or unlearn overnight either. It's an
ongoing process.

It's about continual learning and being open to discussing and
addressing things as they arise. You can, of course, do some
preparation work by researching and reading but, as we know,
children and teenagers are very much their own people and not always
predictable. You can't always anticipate what is going to arise. It's also
fine to not know all the answers, and to give yourself time to process
things and ask for help, whether that be from a partner, family member
or friend.

A misconception about having children is that they don't 'see colour or
racial difference'. How many times have you seen a picture circulating
on social media depicting a white child and a Black child hugging with
a Dr Martin Luther King Jr quote implying that children accept everyone
and are essentially 'colour-blind'? The colour-blind approach often
comes from a position of wanting to treat everyone the same and
therefore not talking about race in the hope of raising non-racist

children. While children can be very accepting in reality, it has been proven that at as young as two or three they start to notice differences in others, such as gender, skin colour, disability and body shapes, and by the age of four or five, they make conscious decisions about their friends and groups.

Children listen to and pick up on messages from us. As their parent or caregiver, you are their most powerful role model. Talking about race from an early age is important so that they understand it's important to you. Talking about race also doesn't have to be about the negative experiences people encounter. It can be a celebration of all the history and great achievements that have been made by BIPOC. There are a plethora of beautiful books, television programmes and films that children can watch to reinforce the positives about having a mixed-race identity.

We spoke to Sandra* again about being a Black mother raising her mixed-race daughter.

Naomi and Natalie: As a Black mother raising a mixed-race child, did you think about it consciously when you fell pregnant that you would be raising a mixed-race child? Or was it something that came after you had your child?

Sandra: I think when my husband and I first got together, the excitement was very much about one day having mixed-race children, but for us it was just an interesting thing to see what they would look like and be like and things like that. We'd been married for, I think, four years before we had our child. So it wasn't anything that we were rushing to do. Then when I was pregnant, it became like a real conscious, 'Right, let's see what we're going to do here,' from her name, to what she wore, how I did her hair, where she was going to live. When I was pregnant, people's obsession with her skin tone came to light – comments like 'I wonder if she's going to be dark?' The fetishisation came in and it became quite overwhelming. As my pregnancy progressed, it definitely became more prevalent.

Naomi and Natalie: We know your child is young, but is there anything that's come up for you (things that maybe you wouldn't think about if you had a monoracial child)?

Sandra: Not so much, but I think that's more because I am with my Black family all the time. If she was seeing her Spanish family, I would think about it more, but essentially, she's being raised as a Black child. I don't really think about it that much because she's not of school age. She's got cousins who are Black and they all just sort of see each other as the same and I think she just sees herself like them.

Growing up in an environment where your identity is different to that of your parents can be confusing particularly if they are uncomfortable or avoid talking about race openly. Remember you can put boundaries in place to protect yourself (see Chapter 6).

Getting comfortable talking about racism, inequality and privilege

Avoiding talking about race because it makes you uncomfortable will undoubtedly lead to problems at some point. You don't have to be an expert and it's fine to acknowledge that there are things you don't know or understand. However, ignoring the racial heritage of your children can lead to other people's ideas framing how your children view themselves (and potentially dangerous narratives). The way you approach this will change depending on the ages of your children. A simple way to approach this is to use the language of fairness, which helps develop empathy. Start talking to children about things in the world that are fair or seem unfair, read books together which opens them up to the worlds of people who aren't like them and equally, if they are the minority in their spaces make sure they see children who look like them represented.

1. **Do not take the colour-blind approach**

   One of the most dangerous things you can do as a parent is take the 'colour-blind' approach. Comments like 'I don't see you as _____' or 'You're not really _____', deny the reality of someone's identity. It won't take long for your children to identify they may look different to you and it's important that they know that is OK. Pretending you don't see or notice this can silently communicate, 'I don't fully see you'.

   In our house, we openly talk to our children about why we all have different skin colours. Because we live in England, we do various things, so they have understanding and appreciation of their Jamaican heritage. At present, my seven-year-old is confident about telling people he is brown and white, but this may change as he gets older.

2. **Ensure your children have role models and people to talk to**

   Your children may well have no one who reflects one or both parts of their heritage in their family. It's important that they have the chance to talk to people and even just experience being around others who look like them.

   I grew up in a household with my two mixed-race sisters and a white mother. My dad lived in Jamaica, so there were no dark-skinned Black people in our home. Our mum would arrange for us to visit our family in Nottingham to ensure we were spending time with our Black family members. I didn't realise it at the time, but it was an intentional act on her part to ensure we understood both sides of our heritage and something I am grateful that she did.

3. **Be aware your children may change the way they identify**
   Identity is fluid. If, for example, you have a white-passing child,
   they may refer to themselves as white, but as they grow up and
   explore other aspects of their identity, they may choose to
   identify as mixed race. You may call your child mixed race but
   as they explore their heritage, they may decide to identify
   monoracially, for example calling themselves Black or brown.
   Siblings may also choose to identify differently. There are many
   factors that could influence the way they identify themselves,
   including their peer group, the school they attend, the area they
   live in and the family members they see most often. Be mindful
   not to project your decision about your child's identity onto them.

4. **Be mindful of the cultural differences in how you will parent**
   Identity and culture will play a huge part in how you choose to
   parent. If you are co-parenting, it's important to have honest
   conversations about things that are important to you and
   expectations you have that the other person may not understand.
   From the food you prepare to the way you dress your children,
   style their hair, practise (or not) any religious beliefs, celebrate
   holidays and the language and parenting styles you use – all
   these are likely to come up. Be aware there may be outside
   pressures from family about decisions you make. For example,
   one family we interviewed told us their white family said they
   shouldn't be talking to their children about racism. My response
   would always be that racism is a reality of our world and it's
   naive to think children won't experience it or pick up on it. If we
   become more open about how it shows up, young people will
   be more empowered and better equipped to challenge it.

5. **Having children may bring up your own issues about identity
   and past experiences**
   For me, having children was a very positive experience in terms
   of my identity. I was determined to ensure they did not grow up

confused or ashamed of their heritage and in turn, it made me embrace my mixedness in a way I hadn't before. If you have suffered trauma or had very difficult experiences, having children may lead you to want to protect them from this. If you have had a bad relationship with one of your parents or they are absent in your life, you may consciously or unconsciously bring that to the table and create a negative perception of that person's whole race rather than just attributing this to the individual. It is important to address these things. Again, having a mixed-race child does not make you immune from racism and prejudice. You may need to do some work to heal from a painful experience or anti-racism work so that you do not pass on that prejudice to your children.

6. **Acknowledge that you will never fully understand their lived experience, but you are always there to support and listen**
Growing up, we experienced racism. This was something our dad had lived with all his life, but we would never fully know how it was to grow up as a dark-skinned Black Jamaican man in 1960s England. Our white mother had lived through microaggressions and seen racism directed towards my father, but would never experience racism herself. Our youngest sister is also much darker-skinned than us and although she identifies as mixed race, her experiences will be with people viewing her as a Black woman. All of our experiences in this world are different, yet we are inextricably linked as family and through love. Our mum has never pretended to understand what we have been through, but she has educated herself so she can be an ally and support us when people are racist or need educating themselves.

7. **Having mixed-race children does not give you a 'free pass'**
You can have mixed-race children and still be racist. And a person can be racist despite having mixed-race children as part

of their wider family. Do not assume that grandparents or aunties and uncles will suddenly become free from racist and xenophobic beliefs because there is now a mixed-race child in the family. If you are reading this and have never read any anti-racism books, now is the time to get started. There are also plenty of articles online to read, Instagram accounts to follow and podcasts you can listen to. If you are unsure where to start there are suggested resources on pp. 219–221.

8. **Make sure your children have access to the things they need in order to have a positive self-image.**
One of the most common things that came up when talking to Black and white mixed-race people about their upbringing was hair. It could be that your children need different hair and skin products from you. Do your research so you know what is most appropriate for them. When we were growing up, we would have to drive to London or get family members to send products to us in the post. The local beauty supplier only had foundation and concealers for white skin tones and there were no hairdressers that knew how to cut and style our hair. Through the internet, you can now get everything you need for your hair type and there are some brilliant independent businesses out there to support. (The Jamii and My Runway Group websites both feature some excellent brands.)

A special thanks to Isla Aitken for her post, 'How to start talking to your kids about racism' for *Everyday Racism*, from which this section was adapted.[3]

One of my most favourite stories from my childhood is watching my mum from the car run across a busy petrol station to catch up with a Black lady who lived locally, but who we did not know back then. Living in a very white-majority area, it was unusual to see Black families. When she got back into the car, I asked her what she was doing. Mum had asked the lady where she got her hair braided and it turned out she did it from home. Later that week, I was sitting on the floor of Veronica's living room having my hair done. Her family became very significant to me. I made friends with her children and it was the first time I had spent time with a Black family who I wasn't related to. Veronica also became a good friend to my mum, who was bringing us up on her own.

Natalie Martello (she/her) is in her mid-thirties and a Muslim woman from London. She is of Jamaican, Irish and English heritage. She is married with five children and identifies as mixed race and Black. She spoke to us about growing up with a white mother and raising her own children.

Natalie M: My mum couldn't do my hair, bless her. I remember it being like a thing where I used to hide the hairbrush down my trousers anytime it was hair time. I used to talk to my friends, and they'd be like, 'Why are you running away with the hairbrush?' I would respond with, 'Because my mum can't brush my hair, it hurts a lot.' I realised that my hair's a bit different to 'Sally's', so maybe hers didn't hurt as much. This was around primary school time because there was a neighbour who lived on the bottom floor of our block of flats, and she ended up sending me to her to get my hair done. So I stopped looking like I was Worzel Gummidge and had decent hair, which was amazing. Then I remember I was maybe three and this little white girl said she didn't want to play with me and some other Black and mixed-race girls because we had rolled in poop. And I was like 'No I haven't; what do you mean?' And she said, 'No, because you're brown, like poo.' I remember being called pic n mix and zebra. Primary school definitely was when I became aware.

Naomi and Natalie: You have five mixed-race children. Have you spoken about identity with your children, or have you allowed them to decide that for themselves?

Natalie M: My husband and I have always explained to them where our parents are from. We have always talked about our heritage. We also try to expose them to it all. My husband loves Jamaican food, so we eat that a lot and we remind the kids that it is their heritage, this is where their granddad came from and that the food is traditional food. I find it difficult to talk about their heritage from their white side, because I don't really know what to cook for that. We've let them gravitate towards whatever it is they show a preference for. They 100 per cent love Jamaican food, culture and when they speak to Granddad (who has a heavy accent because he was born in Jamaica and came over in the 1950s), they love to try to speak in Patois.

They are very proud of their Blackness and are a part of the Black Lives Matter movement. My eldest is taking part in her school newspaper. She did an article with her Somali friend who is dark-skinned about Black Lives Matter. She said in the article, people see her and they're like, 'Oh, who's this white girl?' but she's proud to be Black. There's a real pride that goes beyond skin colour because she's light-skinned. She knows that it doesn't mean she can't be proud to be who she is. I've spoken to her about the fact that her younger sister is probably going to have a very different experience because she's darker and she's probably going to experience things that my eldest doesn't. She says she will speak up for her sister; I've got no doubt she will. We've spoken to them about racism from early on, so they're very passionate about anti-racism work. If you asked them where they are from, not one of them would say, 'Oh, I'm English'. It would probably be an afterthought, they were born here, but they like to say they are Jamaican. I've allowed them to identify as they choose.

Susan (she/her) is in her mid-thirties and is the mother of two children and lives in Scotland. She is white and her daughters are mixed race – one of her daughters is of white British and Punjabi Indian heritage, and her other daughter is white British and Black Jamaican.

Naomi and Natalie: When having mixed-race children, was this something that you thought consciously about when you were pregnant?

Susan: I thought about it a lot. I think because my first child's dad is Indian, and he experienced a lot of xenophobia. The 'foreigner' narrative was thrown around a lot. When I was pregnant, people would ask if the dad was that 'foreign guy', and we would get little microaggressions. I hadn't really prepared for this, but it was one of the things I was more prepared for when I had my second child. I knew that it would be different with her as well because I anticipated that Amelia would not be white passing like her big sister. I expected that we/she would be likely to experience more aggressive xenophobia/racism, anti-Black racism specifically. Lots of things happened at the time when my first child was born that I didn't realise was wrong or inappropriate. For example, when my first child was born, they gave her the TB (tuberculosis) jab, which they do for some kids and when I asked why, they said, 'Oh her dad's from India'. I remember thinking but he doesn't have TB. It felt like they assumed I didn't know her father. I didn't say anything at the time, but I wonder if they would have done that to two white British parents. I also feel like they don't explain these things to you. Similarly with my second child, when she was born in the hospital, she had a blue spot.

Naomi and Natalie: Natalie had a slate grey nevus (formerly known as a Mongolian blue spot). They can look like bruising. They are common among people who are of Asian, Native American, Hispanic, East Indian, and African descent. They are a type of birthmark that doesn't always stay on the skin. Natalie doesn't have hers anymore.

Susan: So, I've always known about it. When my youngest was born, she had one and the nurse pointed it out. I said to her, 'Why do they have that?' I was referring to the medical reasons for why and what it actually was. She said to me in a very condescending tone, 'Oh well, because she's mixed race,' and then laughed and walked away. I was livid and I said nothing. My sister was there at the time and didn't get why I was angry. It was just so ignorant of the nurse to say that. It clearly wasn't what I was asking. If she was a white baby with those strawberry marks and I said, 'Why do they get them?' she would have never said, 'Well, she's a white baby,' and walked away.

Naomi and Natalie: Do you have any examples of how you have tried to encourage the girls' heritage at home?

Susan: It was a lot easier when me and the father of my first daughter were together. It's really just working together. We decided that we could use both languages at home, so I learned a little bit of Punjabi. Her father would always speak to her in Punjabi.

Food is also so important. Food is a cultural signifier, so it is very important. Music as well. We would listen to all kinds of music. That's really important because these things from that young age, they might not specifically remember, but it's going into them. I think it's different for everyone. It depends on the culture as well as how easy or difficult that's going to be compared to where you're living, and the support around you. Where I lived, it was really easy to find Indian ingredients for food. Where I live now, it would be quite difficult. Getting the wider family involved is important as well.

We spoke again to Sushmita, who is raising three mixed-race children. Two are of white British and Korean heritage and one is white British and Indian.

Naomi and Natalie: Can we talk about the impact on your parenting now that you are raising mixed-race children?

Sushmita: I think I am more protective, not necessarily physically, but around their mental health. I'm aware of that and how I'm very sensitive to how people have conversations around them. I try to have conversations with my kids that I wouldn't have to if they were white. Our understanding of what we are trying to say when we say, 'Your skin is beautiful,' is that tangible sense of understanding that, of course, brown is beautiful. It's giving them the extra feeling a little bit more, you know, so that if someone spills something out, we've already filled it back up, so they're never running low. You know, that is so, so important.

We spoke again to Isaac and Emma who are raising a mixed-race child in London.

Naomi and Natalie: Isaac, as a Black parent, what are some of the things you've considered in raising a mixed-race child?

Isaac: I think I was probably reflecting on my own Blackness at the time. I think that's why I was probably quite strong on our child embracing their Black side. I was aware that mixed-race children in society are often seen as Black. I was going super hard on that when really, it's way more nuanced. What really helped my view was speaking to some of my mixed-race friends and them saying stuff to me like, 'Yeah, I relate more to my Black side, but then when I'm around my Black family at Christmas, I feel like I'm not Black enough. And then when I'm around, like my white family, I feel like I'm not white enough.' That gave me more compassion to the fact that even though society will see [my child] as Black and I need to prepare him for that, I don't need to brush his white side under the carpet, because it's still an important part of who he is. I'll just always have this insecurity because we live in England – but it's going to be really easy for him to connect with his white side. But I don't think that's the case, actually. Speaking to mixed-race friends, some of them still find it hard to connect to their white side.

Emma: We had some really intentional conversations before Ezra was born but now he's here, we realised that it's a lot different than talking in hypotheticals. I think a lot of it will be watching him grow and helping to empower him in whatever circles or situations he's in because in reality, we don't want to put pressure on him and say, 'You got to do this the "Black way" or the "white way".' I just want him to feel free and be knowledgeable about all parts of his culture.

Naomi and Natalie: Do you both have any advice or tips to people raising mixed-race children?

Emma: In terms of the cultural side of things and bringing our cultures together, one of my tips would be – and Isaac has taught me this, but as a white person – if you're living in this country, you don't need to push your culture because my culture isn't really one that needs protecting. I am not going to say 'right, we're having fish and chips today and roast tomorrow,' as it's just not necessary. I think for me it's less about pushing my own culture and combining our cultures but it's more about me to embrace and push more for Isaac's culture rather than mine. It doesn't always have to be a 50/50 split.

We spoke to Michael again about what it was like being raised by two white parents.

Naomi: Michael, you have quite a unique experience in terms of being in a family of transracial adoption and being brought up by two white parents. Did you feel like you were quite aware of that from early on?

Michael: Yes, although I guess I wasn't asking those questions. It was very much put to me that I was unique, special. I was born in 1981. Through doing research and as I've grown up later in life, I found out I wasn't actually legally adopted till 1984 because of the challenges they faced [in] wanting to adopt a Black child. I suppose for me, I always felt great pride in them for adopting me. Recently, certain things that have come out which they have been reluctant to tell me, which I suppose, caused a little bit of an issue when you start to think about the identity side of things. For example, there's a sensitive nature to my adoption from Chad and a lot of the story hasn't been straight and it hasn't been as easy to say this is who I am, and where I come from. Some of my adopted family have filled the gap by tracing and meeting their birth parents, whereas for me it's been nigh on impossible for many reasons so that's a bit of an issue. My mum and dad have always been open about the situation. I would get picked up from school by my dad and kids would ask, 'Is that your dad?' It's been quite hard for my parents to explain the whole story and so around ten years ago before I got married, I tried to investigate a little bit more. I got rejected when trying to trace my birth mother (government blocked) so it's quite a fascinating story that I need to explore in more detail as well.

Naomi: Your parents were open about your adoption, and that was something you could talk about. What about in terms of race and growing up? Were there times when that was difficult? Did you feel like you could talk to them? Were there challenges?

Michael: I think there were challenges. There's a lot that I could ask my brother and sister. If I was an only child, it would be a bit different because, you know, let's be honest, they couldn't understand where I was coming from. My uncle married a West Indian lady and they have quite a large West Indian extended family. You go to family parties, you find us all together sharing stories because, like I say, there is that instant thing. You just engage with someone of the same race, you don't need to have to say something. I feel even broaching certain subjects with my parents put them in a very uncomfortable situation and one in which they probably would have cut the conversation off quite quickly. So I went out and did my research. I read lots and lots of books about identity.

I found myself when I was at university at freshers' week and I moved to Twickenham. I was in a house with people who were from Hackney, a Ghanaian guy who was sofa-surfing and another Nigerian guy. Very quickly I went from a very white-centred environment, into a house full of Black guys. That gave me something I'd never experienced before; they looked at me like the white guy, which was very interesting. It was about not being accepted from both sides; I was suddenly the Black guy who played hockey and I was being invited to learn about other people's culture. I learned more about my identity in those six weeks than I had done in twenty years. I felt as though I could ask whatever I wanted to the guys I lived with, whereas growing up it was always coming from a place of we will tell you what you want to hear about your background, but if you ask questions, we won't be that comfortable answering those we don't know the answers to.

Naomi: What things have you had to think about raising your children?

Michael: To be inquisitive; asking questions is really, really important. How I understand my identity is through learning, growing, development and actually, through reflection. I've got a seven-year-old and a four-year-old. I don't think they've experienced too much racism, but unfortunately, it's a reality as they get older. I need to embrace that reality. I'm not going to shelter them from anything because that just leads to more questions.

Reflections for Parents:

1. How does it make you feel that your children may have a different racial identity to you?
2. How have you prepared yourself to help your children understand both or all parts of their racial identity?
3. Where are the gaps and how might you need to educate yourself so you can meet their needs?
4. In what ways might you have ignored both, or all parts of their identity?
5. What anti-racism work have you done or are currently undertaking to ensure you are addressing any conscious or unconscious bias?
6. As a parent have you ever played down issues around race raised by your children because you felt uncomfortable?
7. How do you celebrate your children's identity in your home?
8. Do your children have role models, or access to people who represent both or all parts of their racial identity? If not, how could you proactively help them to have others in their life that they can relate to?

Chapter 9

'Oh my god, can I touch your hair?':

On mixed-race hair

~~~

Natalie: The question 'Can I touch your hair?' might not sound particularly distressing in isolation, but for many of us reading this, it might send shivers down the spine or evoke memories of being made to feel like some sort of animal at the petting zoo. Well, at least they asked, you might say. However, it's never actually a genuine question because usually by the time you hear it, the other person's hands are already stroking your hair.

From my earliest memories, I remember people touching my hair. I can recall once looking up and seeing a smiling white woman who looked ecstatic to see me. Her hand reached in and she grabbed, stroked and pulled my hair with a delighted expression and made an ignorant comment. As I got older, it wasn't only white women who touched my hair. White men felt they had the right to step into my personal space and touch me. I believe this to be a mix of curiosity, as well as the beginning of being sexualised once I was in my late teens. This sense of violation still affects me to this day.

According to Gary Chapman, author of 1992 book *The Five Love Languages*,[1] there are five primary love languages: words of affirmation, quality time, physical touch, acts of service, and receiving gifts. For me, physical touch is always last. I don't like people hugging me, putting their hand on my shoulder or anyone going near my hair. When people get close to me, I tense up. I retreat like a tortoise in its shell; I want the ground to swallow me up. It's because throughout my whole life, people have crossed my boundaries. There have been those who have inserted themselves into my personal space and stepped over a line that shouldn't have ever been crossed. Again and again, being perceived as 'different', 'unique' or 'intriguing' has meant having to navigate microaggressions, dehumanising situations and comments from people who repeatedly chose to satisfy their curiosity without any regard for my feelings.

In August 2021 a white Irish broadcaster, Eamonn Holmes, who presents the popular ITV breakfast show *This Morning*, was in conversation with regular contributor Dr Zoe Williams, who is a mixed-race woman. Discussing an upcoming segment about how our health can benefit from contact with animals he looked at her hair and said, 'Your hair reminds me of an alpaca . . . You just want to pet it, don't you? It's very alpaca-ish.' Following a barrage of complaints he released an apology: 'Hey everyone out there. If my attempt at being humorous with my friend Dr Zoe Williams was misjudged, I am mortified and humbly apologise to anyone who was offended.'[2]

This sort of comment will be familiar to those of us with non-Eurocentric standards of hair. To some it's an 'innocent' joke but the roots of these comparisons to animals and entitlement to freely touch non-white bodies goes much deeper. The objectification of Black people and our bodies is nothing new and is a continuation from slavery. The commodification of African slaves was not only linked to the free labour that was expected, but the sexual objectification that was prominent during the slavery era, specifically towards African American women. Black women were seen as subhuman and compared to animals with sexual appetites. Sarah Baartman, who was born in 1789, was a Black South African woman who was sexually objectified for her large buttocks. She was brought to Europe by a British doctor and exhibited for 'freak shows'. Even after she died in 1815 her skeletal remains and sexual organs were displayed in a museum in Paris until 1974. People view her today as an archetype of colonial racism and exploitation, and an example of the harm caused by stereotypes, objectification and sexualisation of Black women.[3]

When we talk about Black bodies, this also refers to Black hair. Stigmatising Black, Afro, curly hair was a way colonisers gained mastery over Black people. Prior to the trans-Atlantic slave trade, hair in many African tribes was seen as a symbol of social status; it could tell you everything about a person. When the first enslaved Africans arrived in colonial Virginia in 1619 (marking the beginning of the trans-Atlantic slave trade), they were forced to have their hair shaved off, which was a dehumanising act.[4] According to the *Merriam-Webster Dictionary*, to dehumanise is 'to deprive (someone or something) of human qualities, personality, or dignity.' In this case, it was a way of demolishing enslaved peoples' identity and to make them feel they were worthless.[5] On the plantations they were forced to work on, Black people had no hair products or tools to use, which resulted in having to find other ways to care for their hair, including utilising items such as axle grease. Enslaved people were often only allowed one designated day to care for their hair. Even in such horrific and sadistic conditions, African people held onto traditions and culture that we still see to this day, such as 'wash day' and braiding of the hair.[6]

In 1786, Louisiana had a free Black population of around 18,000. The Spanish Governor of Louisiana, Esteban Rodríguez Miró, recognised a 'growing sensitivity of the white population' towards Black people alongside a 'growing mixed population', so sought to put in place more restrictive and confining laws to 'control its progressiveness'. The introduction of the Tignon laws discouraged 'Plaçage' (relationships between white men and free women of colour, also known as Creole women – women of European, usually French or Spanish and African descent). During this time Black and mixed-race women wore their hair in elegant and extravagant ways, adorning it with feathers and jewels, which attracted a lot of white male attention. This deeply concerned white women as it contributed to a rise in interracial relationships and an increase in mixed-race children that subsequently 'threatened' the class status of white women. The Tignon laws prohibited Black and mixed-race women from showing their hair. It was also enforced to ensure that regardless of whether they were enslaved or not, they would know that they belonged to a class system.[7]

Even with the Tignon laws in place, Black and mixed-race women continued to own their style. In 1803 the Tignon laws were abolished but many free and enslaved women continued covering their hair as a statement and an act of protest. By the early nineteenth century, Black women discovered the hot comb, a metal straightening comb which was heated to operate much like an iron, using heat to comb out waves and curls. It was first marketed in the 1800s as a tool to enable Black and mixed-race women to access European standards of hair. It was also around this time that Madam C. J. Walker became the first Black millionaire after she developed hair products which revolutionised the hair industry.[8]

Times have dramatically changed and as of late, embracing natural hair is seen as a revolutionary act. More and more women are learning how to style and look after their curls, kinks, coils and Afros. According to a study carried out by market research firm Mintel between 2012 and 2017, sales of relaxers dropped by 38 per cent.[9] With more and more representation in the media, from Solange's hit single, 'Don't Touch My Hair' to Emma Dabiri's book of the same name, for many, the choice to go natural is a political statement. We're refusing to buy into the Eurocentric idea of beauty standards and our hair doesn't need to be changed for us to fit in. That said, many Black and mixed-race women still choose to wear their hair straight, with the operative word being 'choose', and not as a necessity for acceptance.

In 2009, Chris Rock's documentary *Good Hair* arrived on our screens prompted by his daughter asking him why she doesn't have 'good hair'.[10] The documentary harshly criticised Black women's hair journeys through their use of relaxers, weaves, and straightening their hair. Though, at times it does raise some key issues, it doesn't give an honest analysis as to why Black women do this to their hair and offers no cogent for change. Even though the natural hair movement has been significantly liberating for many, for others, wearing their hair however they please, including straightening or a weave can be equally empowering. What matters is the autonomy to wear your hair however you choose without fear of discrimination or judgement. My current hairdresser is Edith, a Nigerian woman whom I spend eight hours with every few weeks watching Nollywood movies back-to-back on YouTube while she braids my hair, and we sip tea with condensed milk. The last time I saw her I relayed how I had been at work and someone had asked to touch my fresh box braids. 'You want to know why they do it?' she said to me. 'Jealousy and intrigue. We are so creative with our hair. We are so clever. All the different ways Black people can style up and change our hair is amazing.' I had to admit I had never felt that way before. To be honest, I often had a sense of embarrassment at the amount of times I changed my style. More often than not I felt distinct apprehension after having my hair done and leaving the house, fearful of the questioning and commentary that would inevitably follow, however innocent or well-meaning. It felt far closer to being in a state of anxiety rather than an expression of creativity.

As Emma Dabiri writes about in her brilliantly enlightening 2019 book, *Don't Touch My Hair*:

> *The Afro-diasporic cultural tendency does not merely copy, rather it innovates, melding old with the new and creating something entirely original in the process. Black women might wear their hair*

straight but that fact alone does not manifest a slavish reproduction of European aesthetics . . . Whatever the style, whatever the social convention or prevailing aesthetic, hairstyling has been an essential component of a strong visual language that has been passed down through the generations across Africa and her diaspora.[11]

For some, the way in which we style our hair can be seen as a type of resistance to white colonialism and white supremacy. For others, it's about seeing more culturally affirming images of themselves and feeling a sense of self-worth. For many, it's given them the ability to live more freely in their own bodies. With this in mind, it's important to always remember that someone touching your hair without permission is not a 'trivial thing'; it's not you being 'over-sensitive'. We have had to fight for centuries to be allowed to embrace our natural hair and white people have continually dictated our styles to us. It's a power trip and most of the time, white people don't even realise what they are doing is seriously problematic. We have every right to redress that power dynamic. If you don't want your hair touched, you have every right to say so.

Hair types

My hair texture is type 3C. It's changed over the years; as a child I had tight coils and now it's much looser and fuller. Hair texture was puzzling to me growing up. There was very little language around it, and most of the time, my hair was simply described as 'frizzy'. In the early 1990s, stylist Andre Walker accidentally created what is now known as the 'hair typing system' which categories hair from the number 1 (being the straightest) up to 4C. He originally created it for his own hair-care products, however, it is now widely used as a hair type classification. Initially it started out with four types: straight, wavy, curly and coily. However, following a chart has major limitations, with many of us having a range of textures on our heads. The hair type system has also created a hierarchical system of what some would perceive as 'good curls' and 'bad curls', which we know as texturism.[12]

Texturism

Writer Zeba Blay discusses texturism in an article for *HuffPost* in which she raises the issue of 'colorism in the natural hair community'.[13] Texturism is the idea that some natural hair patterns are more attractive than others. Essentially, looser, softer curls (known as type 3) are deemed more desirable because they are positioned in closer proximity to whiteness and Eurocentric beauty standards. Those with coarser hair are more likely to be subjected to prejudicial treatment and hair discrimination. Again this is very much a legacy of the trans-Atlantic slave trade. Words attributed to textured hair such as 'bad' or 'rough' and no access to tools that would enable people to care for their hair was another way to dehumanise Black people.

My hair very much lived up to this 'good hair' trope. People would be drawn to me like a magnet in the street, saying phrases like, 'I wish I had curly hair like you, it's beautiful.' My response would be, 'I wish I had straight hair.' They would usually respond with a chuckle and say something like, 'I guess we always want what we can't have right?' Now, when I think about this phrase, I realise how troublesome it is. I never actually wanted straight hair, it was never about having 'something we can't have', it was a feature that I had been conditioned into desiring. I wanted my hair to be accepted. I love my hair, I love my coils, I love that when I pull my curl down it bounces back into place, I love that the ends of my hair go blonde in the summer, I love my ritual of using a deep nourishing conditioner and having a combing-out day. I absolutely love that I only have to wash my hair once a week. So, why straight hair? What I learned was that those with straighter hair and lighter skin gained more opportunities. Straight hair was seen as less 'hassle', easier to style, and of course, it was what I saw in every magazine and on every billboard, film and TV show. Straight hair is what every single one of my friends had, so at sleepovers, when we would do each other's hair, it's what I wished I had so I could join in. Straight hair was the only hair type that the hairdressers I went to knew how to style. I wished I had straight hair, not because I preferred it, but because it felt easier.

For many mixed-race people, understanding and loving our hair is a journey, particularly if you live in a place as a minority. Today, we are seeing more appreciation for natural hair and there are so many more accessible products, information and understanding than there was when we were growing up. I am wholeheartedly grateful to those who have documented their journey and hair routines, particularly online, to show us how it's done.

One of my earliest memories when it comes to my own hair journey was when my mum would try and detangle my hair. When you have type 3 hair and you wear it down all day, it tends to knot, so it's important to comb these out. She tried her hardest to ensure it didn't hurt while she detangled the knots. She would section each part and lightly comb it, usually while it was dry. I remember once when my dad was visiting from Jamaica, he was watching her do my hair. His face looked confused as he said, 'That's not how you do Black hair. You need to be firmer; you need to toughen up her scalp, here let me show you.' Those ten minutes I will never forget. I can still feel the pain; the feeling that someone is pulling your hair so hard that your scalp might fall off. He wasn't holding the top of my hair as he brushed it, so it was excruciating. I don't blame either of my parents for that incident because I know what they were trying to achieve. On one hand, my mum was trying to be gentle and comb it out how she thought was best and on the other hand, my dad was trying to treat my hair like the other Black women he had watched when he was younger, sitting in the hair salons while my nana spent hours having her hair detangled and then straightened with a hot iron. What neither of them realised is that my hair is different from what either of them knew.

No one knew how to do my hair. I went to countless white hairdressers who looked like rabbits in headlights every time I walked in and when I would travel up to London to go to a Black hairdresser, I would think to myself, *Great, they will know what they are doing*, but again, they didn't. The products used on my hair were way too strong, and they would either burn my hair or I would have allergic reactions to them. I remember being under the dryer and it burning my scalp because it was too hot, and being too young and nervous to tell them, as the other Black women next to me seemed to be fine.

When I reached my teenage years, I warmly welcomed the relaxer into my life. Finally, I could 'control' my hair and blend in with other people. No one would try to touch it, and I would look like everyone else. For the next twelve years, I straightened my hair. It's sad because when I look back, I realise these messages were internalised, but I didn't analyse why. I believe now it came from a place of internalising anti-Black notions, not wanting to stand out and the need to be in closer proximity to whiteness. There was one point in my teenage years where I decided to go natural and that was after the 2002 film *Austin Powers in Goldmember* came out – I was thirteen years old. I still reminisce about the memory of Beyoncé in her gold bikini, with her Afro hair, playing the one and only Foxxy Cleopatra. To me, this confidence felt revolutionary. I recall thinking, 'I can get my hair like that,' so I did. For a whole three days, I brushed my hair out to make it into an Afro. I braided the front of my hair to the side and walked around with pride. I remember being at a family BBQ and my cousin said to me, 'Wow, I love your hair, you look amazing.' I was bursting with happiness; however, this feeling didn't last long because as soon as school came around, those feelings of insecurity soon arose. Everyone at school looked at me as I walked down the corridor, my hair was fondled by many hands, followed by comments of 'Oh wow, you look like [. . .]' and there I was again, back home straightening my hair once more.

When I was fourteen, I decided I wanted box braids. I had previously had my hair braided but not with extensions before. After the longest twelve hours of my life, a very sore head and a numb bum, my hair was complete. I cannot explain how much I loved it. I was so excited to go to school the next day and show off my new braids to my friends. The next day went exactly as planned. Everyone LOVED my new hairstyle. I was getting stopped in the hallway, people were staring at me and telling me how much they liked it. I was ecstatic. Later that day, I got called to the headteacher's office. I had no idea why and walked down the long corridor with my heart pounding. I knocked on the door. 'Come in,' he said. Our Head was a very scary man; you didn't mess with him. I sat down and he proceeded to tell me that my hair was against the school rules, that it was distracting other pupils and that I must take it out before school the next day. My heart sank. Distracting? Take it out? Did he not realise how long it would take me to undo all these plaits? I went home in tears and told my mum everything. She was not happy. She reassured me that I would not be taking my hair out and she would be at the school the following morning to talk to him.

Usually, I would beg her not to go to the school. You see, our mum was at our school most weeks challenging something ambiguous, but on this occasion I didn't mind. The next day, I sat outside the Head's office and heard my mum with a raised voice asking him to explain how my hair went against school rules and telling him how braids were a part of my heritage and how disgustingly racist it was to tell me I couldn't wear my hair in this style. Needless to say, I got to keep my box braids in.

Stories like this are not unusual and hair discrimination has been happening for years. In 2020, Ruby Williams was sent home from her school in east London for breaching hair policy which stated that 'Afro-style hair must be of reasonable size and length'.[14] We now have incredible organisations such as the Halo Code who are an alliance of organisations and individuals working to create a future without hair discrimination. Now schools can adopt this hair code to ensure they are no longer discriminating against Afro-textured hair and styles.

Fast-forward a few years, and I discovered weaves and hair glue. Because there were no Black hairdressers in the area, my sister and I learned how to do each other's hair. We were self-taught and became pretty skilled. Endless nights of washing, drying, straightening, then parting and glueing in the weave. It would take a lot of time and planning. Over the years, we discovered the best weave to order online, and Remi hair was our go-to. Wash day was an event. I would pull the weave out, drench my hair in a conditioner, wash the weave and hang it on the washing line. Then it was time to brush out the hair glue, which was the worst. I remember working for my local church at the time. We were running a charity event and looking for ways to raise money. It was suggested that I wear my hair in an Afro for two weeks and people could sponsor me and being very naive, I agreed. At the time I thought it was a bit of fun, similar to how people shave off their hair for charity. I was just doing my part, right? Now looking back I see how problematic that was. Wearing my hair naturally was turned into a spectacle, an anomaly, a 'brave' thing to do, so much so that people would give me money to do it.

191

It isn't unusual for Afro hair to be ridiculed; it's been the butt of the joke for years, from golliwogs with their 'frizzy hair' to minstrels' woolly hair. Back in 2016, it came to light that when you googled 'unprofessional hairstyle for work', the image results would show Black women with natural hair. When you searched for professional hairstyles, the image results would show white women with straight hair. We have had to put up with implicit and explicit bias towards our hair that is ingrained not only online, but also in places such as the workplace, schools or universities.[15] We still have a long way to go when it comes to people's implicit and explicit biases towards Afro-textured hair.

Sophie Williams (she/her) is the author of two books, *Millennial Black* and *Anti-Racist Ally*. Sophie's mother is Black Jamaican, and her father is white British. She identifies as a Black woman and she shared with us experiences she's had with her hair.

Naomi and Natalie: Can you tell us a little about your hair journey?

Sophie: I guess I probably first got my hair relaxed in primary school and I don't think I had it like that often, but I think definitely from about twelve, my hair was relaxed until the end of university.

Naomi and Natalie: Did you ask for your hair to be relaxed?

Sophie: Yeah, I guess so. My sister's older than me. She is much darker-skinned and she's not mixed race. She always had her hair in braids and that's not something that I ever really had. I remember her saying to my mum that she shouldn't send me to school with my natural hair because people will think she didn't take care of me, in the same way that we saw with the comments people made about [Beyoncé and Jay-Z's daughter] Blue Ivy when she was little. The question would always be, 'Is my hair tidy enough?'

Remember how little girls used to have big plaits with big hair bobbles on the ends of their hair? Well, I had that in primary school and then I relaxed it by the time I was at secondary school. The problem with relaxed hair is it's really restrictive, because you can't do things your friends are doing. Going swimming, having a water or snowball fight, or even exercising can 'ruin' your hair. It's a massive weight and it was so restrictive. I remember living in Paris and I was teaching English to someone who had really straight hair and she would always tell me how her hair was really curly, and that she would use this product she'd got online to straighten her hair. It was an unregulated product, it turns out – but I decided to use it. You put the product, this strong smelling liquid, into the hair while it's still wet and then you have to blow-dry it to really pull it straight. The reason the product was unregulated was that it's actually full of formaldehyde, and as soon as I put heat on my hair, my nose started bleeding. Not just a trickle. A huge pouring of blood. But I wanted straight hair so much that I just thought to myself, *it's worth it, don't worry; this is going to look so good. It's going to swish about like hair on TV!* I did that around five or six times, buying the same stuff on the internet, putting it on my hair and bleeding immediately, but I carried on thinking to myself, *it's worth it.*

I used to be really conscious of how I wore my hair to jobs and job interviews, so whichever way I wore my hair to interviews, in my first week on the job, I would always try to make sure that I wore my hair another way (just so it didn't become a 'big thing' later). When I used to wear my hair straight and then go into work one day with it curly, people would say, 'Wow I didn't recognise you.' I also wondered, 'Why? I have got the same face – it doesn't make sense.'

If anyone touches my hair, I still put my hands right in their hair because, if it's not a comfortable thing for me to do to you, then it's not a comfortable thing for you to do to me. I've had so many people who touch my hair and say, 'Oh, it's just so nice,' and I just want to scream, 'Get off my body now!' I have very little tolerance for that kind of nonsense. Before going to events or things where I don't know who's going to be there, but my partner does, I have to ask, 'Is everyone briefed? Is anyone going to touch me?' or, 'Will I be the only person like me there?' I think we have to have that sort of thought that white people just don't have to spend the mental energy thinking about.

Naomi: I just had a flashback of our old boss at work. He would come over to me and say, 'Is that a weave?' or, 'You got a weave in today?' I would laugh along, and it was always so public, in front of everyone.

Sophie: And that certainly shouldn't be from someone who you don't have that personal relationship with because what I don't think we're saying is you could never talk to us about our hair or having a conversation about hair is off limits. What I am saying though is, my general rule is that you can talk to me, and I can talk to you, about something that you've chosen today. So, if you have put on a really nice jumper or you've done something really kind, I would talk to you about that. The texture of my hair is always here and it's not up for conversation. This is my weight, this is my body, always, and it's not up for conversation – I didn't choose that today. I will only talk to people about something that they've made a conscious choice to have as part of their day. And we have to remember that power differential, whether it's a boss or teachers etc. It isn't an even relationship where you can say, 'I don't want to talk about this.' It is putting you in a situation that you haven't asked for, with someone who is controlling elements of your income or education.

Aaliyah* (she/her) identifies as mixed race. Her dad is Black Trinidadian, and her mum is white German. She is in her mid-twenties and was born and raised in a central European country and moved to

the UK when she was eighteen and has lived here ever since. She spoke to us about how she felt about her hair growing up and what that's like now.

Naomi and Natalie: Could you tell us about your hair journey? How do you feel about your hair generally and how did you feel growing up when it comes to your hair?

Aaliyah: As a child, I hated my hair. I'm still on that spectrum. Currently, I don't love my hair, but I'm just trying to get there. If you'd spoken to me a year ago, my hair would have been completely straight. From a very young age, I hated it. I used to have cornrows done and then people would make fun of my scalp and I hated it. My brother has wavy hair, and my dad is bald, so I don't have any examples of really nice curly hair. I got my hair chemically straightened when I was about thirteen all the way up to two years ago. Because I grew up in a predominantly white country and environment, when I moved to the UK at eighteen, it really changed my perspective because you see so many different people who are different ethnicities, especially living in London. It kind of took me on a journey of discovering my Black side. I was talking to my brother about this recently and we never really talked about it when we were younger. We have family in Trinidad, but we didn't think about the culture that much. It was a very white culture that we grew up in. When I came to the UK, I started to realise that I liked curly hair. I could see it on these girls, and I would think, *I know my hair can look like that*. I also found that my workplace was much more relaxed. It wasn't a corporate environment. I felt comfortable having my hair curly at work.

Naomi and Natalie: Did you feel that straightening your hair for work or working in corporate environments was a smarter look than your natural hair?

Aaliyah: Yes, definitely. My dad would always tell me curly hair doesn't look tidy; it looks messy. So, from a young age I'd be like, I don't want to show my curls because it doesn't look formal. We've all had those moments when your parents would do your hair and pull your scalp and I would hate it so much, I would scream.

Naomi and Natalie: When you discovered that you wanted to go natural, what did you do to understand how to style your hair or how to manage it?

Aaliyah: I don't actually know. Basically, the first thing I did was to stop straightening it and just stop getting the chemical treatment. I know my curl pattern and I did watch some YouTube videos that would tell me which brush to use but I already knew what was working for me. Then some of my friends would say, 'Oh I know this place that specialises in curly hair.' Instagram was a huge help and a place where I felt influenced with and saw styles that I could do. And they had reels I could watch, and I thought, I can do that.

Naomi and Natalie: When you lived at home, did you do your own hair? Did you ever go to the hairdressers, or did you just stay at home and do it yourself?

Aaliyah: My dad would go to the Black hair shop; I wouldn't even go. He would just come back with loads of products and just hand them to me, and I would do my thing, or he would try and help, but it would hurt. My mum never really ventured into the hair journey. We had Nigerian friends and sometimes my parents would ask them to do my hair, maybe braid it or something, but other than that I did everything else on my own.

We spoke again to Isla and she shared with us her experiences of embracing her natural hair.

Natalie and Naomi: We've all had a hair journey. What would you say yours has looked like since you were younger?

Isla: It's been interesting, I didn't realise that my hair was different to my mum's for a long time, and so I would say to her, 'Oh, I really want extensions. I really want it relaxed.' She would say, 'No, no, no, you don't need to have it done, because that's only for people who've got shorter hair.' I just didn't really get it. There was one time when she had it texturised. It wasn't chemically straightened, but she did have something done to it, so the texture was slightly different. I thought, well why can't I do it, or why can't I even straighten it? I guess for me it wasn't an option, which it often is for many Black girls and at a certain age you go and get your hair relaxed because then it's 'manageable'. My hair texture meant that it wasn't 'necessary'. I think my hair texture is 2B.

Natalie and Naomi: What are your thoughts on the hair-texture chart?

Isla: I don't mind it because it sometimes helps in terms of identifying products that can be helpful to use. With social media, if you start following someone who has similar hair texture, it's helpful in that way.

Francis Galton was a eugenicist and scientific racist who believed in the inferiority of the Black Africans and used hair texture as one signifier of this. He had a little case that had different hair types in it, and your proximity to whiteness was judged by your hair texture and again, its classification by hair type. That's obviously not what we're doing by deciding whether we're 4C or 2B because I think what we're doing is just understanding our hair and celebrating it and embracing it in its natural state. It is very different, but again, it's just that kind of categorisation. Right at the beginning of the natural hair movement, it really started gaining traction on social media. Women whose natural hair were looser curly hair textures, we were kind of fawning over and

celebrating and being like, 'Oh, wow, yeah, maybe I'll do it too.'
However, this texture is slightly removed from Afro-textured hair.

I started experimenting really with my hair when I went to the
Dominican Republic. Hair is massive in all Black communities, but
Dominicans are really well known in America for example, in New
York, where they own a lot of the salons. They're just sort of known for
their hair and their products and their techniques. I really got into that
quite a lot when I was there and was around eighteen years old. I had
my first roller-set hair blow-dry experience and was able to swish my
hair, it was very special. I also had my first accidental relaxer
experience. I went to a salon thinking, *I'm just getting a blow-dry*, and
on it went, and it started to burn. I didn't know they were going to do
that. I think they were just trying to get extra money for their friend who
owned the salon and me being a foreigner with considerably more
disposable income than they did, they tried it on me. I thought I looked
very different with straight hair and I didn't love it. Prior to that I would
just scrape my hair out the way. It was frizzy and I didn't really know
what to do with it. Now, it has kind of become a part of my everyday
life, like I was actually thinking about what to do with it. When I left the
Dominican Republic, I moved to London and again, had access to more
products, more Black friends, more than I'd had when I was living in
Kent as a child, so it was again another experience of building a
relationship with my hair. Then after university, I started to regularly
straighten it but just with straightening irons or rollers and blow-dry.
That was my look for a long time.

Natalie and Naomi: Can you tell us a little about your hair routine?

Isla: Trial and error. So much trial, not that much error, because I'm not
doing anything chemical, other than bleaching at times, which I've
regretted. I use as few products as I can, but I know that the general

consensus behind curly hair is that you don't use products with sulphates in them and often shampoos have a lot of sulphates in, so I've chosen products that don't have sulphates in them. I can't resist shampooing just because I use a lot of oil-based products like pure coconut oil and that's the main thing that I use really regularly, so I am guilty of shampooing. I'll wash it once a week at most. This was the same when I was younger, and my mum would wash my hair and grease my scalp. I was doing that for a long time but then I read somewhere that greasing your scalp isn't always the best thing to do, so I stopped. I just put grease in my hair just to keep [it] hydrated because, you know, living by the sea in the salty air, it feels dry quite a lot. I kind of trial different products and because I'm vegan, I only go for cruelty-free products that are free from animal-derived ingredients.

Natalie and Naomi: Do you have many 'Don't touch my hair' moments?

Isla: I haven't had loads to be honest. I have had it touched if I've had it in elaborate styles or I've done it differently one day at work then people will be like, 'Oh wow!' and just grab a hold. There have been occasions where I've gone along with it just because it was so normal in supposedly comfortable spaces, for example: the workplace where people will be like, 'Oh, I really like your top,' but they won't touch you, but for them to then transfer it to your body (which your hair is part of), it took me a moment to react. I've always worked in predominantly white spaces. I'm really conscious of being the only person, so I think I've just inherited that wanting to be the 'good, palatable Black friend'.

Natalie and Naomi: What would be your advice if someone was saying this keeps happening to them?

Isla: There was one occasion when it happened, and I played out in my head how I would react if it ever happened to me again. I basically said to myself, 'just grab a hold of their hair and just see how they react.' You can just say, 'Oh, well I thought that's just what we were doing?', and then you can start that conversation because I think we all know about white fragility and calling these things out and how that plays out for Black and brown women because you're then branded as the 'troublemaker'. You're the one who's made the issue out of 'nothing'. Doing it in a tactful way was important for me, especially in the workplaces that I found myself in.

There was one occurrence, which I found very strange. I was standing behind the counter of the place that I worked at the time and a colleague was crouched down nearby. As she stood up, she brushed my hair with her arm or something and she jumped back and said, 'Oh, get your fuzzy hair away from me.' I don't even remember reacting or saying anything. I probably apologised and I think about that instance a lot. It just made me really sad and angry because it was an awful experience and yet I felt I needed to apologise.

How you can respond when someone touches your hair without asking:

1. 'Please do not touch my hair; I don't like it.'
2. 'I'm not quite sure why you think it's OK to touch my hair but don't do that again.'
3. 'I really don't know where your hands have been and the last time you washed them, so please don't put them in my hair.'
4. Return the gesture; put your hands in their hair and see what they say.

What not to say about Black hair:

1. 'Have you got a weave?'
2. 'Why are you always changing your hair?'

3. 'I was only giving you a compliment!'
4. 'I wouldn't mind if people touched my hair.'
5. 'Is your hair natural?'
6. 'I wish I had curly hair like you; I hate my hair, it's so boring.'
7. 'It's just hair.'

How to support children with their natural hair:

1. Invest in the right products. It's not always as simple as buying products from the local chemist or supermarket. Research what products are best for your child's hair type.
2. All hair is different. Don't make assumptions.
3. Show them positive images of people with hair like theirs.
4. Ensure they don't have to put up with problematic comments or behaviours towards their hair.

Chapter 10

Reflections:

Things I want to tell my younger self about racial identity

~~

'You don't have to change to fit one or the other, you are both, and that's OK. You don't have to try so hard to impress or prove to people, "but I'm Black" or "I'm white". Just be who you are because who you are is good enough.'
Natalie M – Identifies as mixed race and Black. She is of Jamaican, Irish and English heritage.

~~~

'All your feelings are valid, but you need to give them context. Like it's OK that I feel isolated or like I'm being discriminated against, but contextually, where does that sit compared to my peers and other people in this group and what they're experiencing and then exercising my frustration from that. Someone discriminating against me is not OK – it needs a response and it needs to be dealt with, but does that compare to the systemic racism that a darker-skinned Black woman has had her entire life? Why is that? Let's have that conversation and contextualise my privilege.'
Kayleigh – identifies as mixed race and is of Black African and white British heritage.

~~~

'I guess I'm quite happy with how things have turned out, so I guess I would say, it's going to be OK. It doesn't always feel like it is. And there isn't always an easy spot in the world for you, but you can make one; you can be intentional about who you let into your life.'
Sophie Williams – identifies as a Black woman. Her mother is Black Jamaican, and her father is white British.

'I think for me, I would say to myself that number one would be to stand up to people more and say how you actually feel. Don't feel embarrassed. That's the main thing, just embrace it and be more proud. Don't be so insecure. That's easier said than done, but that's kind of what I would probably tell myself, like, you're going to love it one day, so you may as well start now.'

Kym – Identifies as mixed race. Her mum is white (British English), and dad East Asian (of Chinese heritage).

~~~

'There was a perception around me that I had "an attitude"; I was a "rude boy", [a] "bad boy" which all had racist undertones. I was always reminded that I had "a chip on my shoulder" and I believe they wanted me to have that chip on my shoulder so they could manipulate that. That "chip" was actually me expressing my culture. I'd say embrace that and wear it with pride. Don't take on that heavy burden that people want to load onto you. It's not a chip; it's a badge of honour. I wish I could have worn it better and represented it better growing up.'

Michael – identifies as Black British. He was adopted at birth and raised by two white parents.

~~~

'I let a lot of the casual racism slide because I thought that I would come across as overreacting or being too sensitive. I would tell myself you have every right if someone's making a point about your race to say you didn't find that funny and didn't think that's OK. I felt like I had to laugh along and think, *oh, it's just a joke; it's not causing me physical harm*, even though it did. I would say to myself, "Don't worry about not seeming like you don't have a sense of humour, it's OK to say this impacts you."'

Courteney – Identifies as mixed race. Her mum is white (British English), and dad East Asian (of Chinese heritage).

~~~

'I would tell myself it's not you. You haven't got it wrong. A lot of the way you are feeling is because of racism, which is not your fault. The images that you look at and the people that you spend time with don't look like you, so it makes you feel inadequate but the world around you will open up and evolve. These feelings won't last forever. You'll start to feel much more a part of things and as you grow in confidence, you'll find your voice and your place in the world. Sometimes these things take time, and the waiting feels painful, but it's part of the process.'

Naomi Evans – Identifies as Black mixed race.

~~~

'Find people who love you for you and don't fight so hard to be in the box created for you.'

Alexis – identifies as a queer woman of colour. She is half-Bajan and half-British.

~~~

'I would tell my younger self to enjoy and relish not knowing. I spent so long really feeling like I wasn't valid until I knew all the answers. I think that that stopped me from stuff. I stopped a lot of self-love. There was a lot of self-hate because I didn't fit easily into a box. So, I would tell my younger self to relish the not knowing and enjoy it. Try and find some

enjoyment in being the other, in being totally unique and someone who no one else is going to be.'
Jacob – identifies as mixed race. He grew up believing he was of Brazilian heritage but discovered later in life he is Guyanese.

~~~

'I would say not to be afraid to be different. It's OK to not fit that mould. Actually, it's quite nice.'
Aaliyah – identifies as mixed race. Her dad is Black Trinidadian, and her mum is white German.

~~~

'I'm very proud of my younger self, of the way that I've always been very self-aware, a fighter and an advocator. Maybe just chill out a little bit, don't be so aggressive with it (but then, they deserved it). Be happy with who you are and love yourself because you only get one chance at this. Don't ever think that you are any less or like you have to choose a side. Just be you, and carry on doing amazing, wonderful work in terms of understanding injustice and oppression and being sensitive to people struggling.'
Michelle – identifies as a Black mixed-race woman. She is of white English, Black Jamaican and Chinese heritage.

~~~

'Accept who you are because your skin colour doesn't define you. I really felt like I didn't belong. I felt like I was fake and like I was placed on a pedestal by society above my mum and my nan. I just felt like it was unfair. Don't blame yourself. That's not in your control.'
Yasmine – identifies as mixed race. She is white and Black African.

'You're fine; you're OK; you're loved; you're enough. When I was younger, wanting to be a princess was quite a big thing and there were no princesses that looked like me. So when *The Princess and the Frog* came out (which is an interesting film and not without its problematic issues), that meant quite a lot to me. So, just reminding my younger self, that, yeah, I'm a princess and I'm Wonder Woman at the same time. I'm strong and I can do whatever I want.'

Isla – identifies as Black and mixed heritage. Her mum was Black Jamaican and her dad was white Scottish.

'I'd say, you're not the problem. You need to understand that the schools haven't been equipped with the right tools. I would tell myself that, and don't be worried about fitting in a certain box. And it's OK to make mistakes. If my younger self knew that I'd go on to write a play about my experiences, that it would be on BBC News and I'd be delivering workshops at schools in Norfolk and Norwich, then I'd say what's happening to you now is going to make you a better person when you're older and it will make you more empathetic towards other people as well.'

Ashton – identifies as Black mixed race.

'Be you. If I had that input when I was younger to just be me, unapologetically me, and just to trust that it'll work out, it would have been a really good support and encouragement for me. I generally didn't feel like I fit in anywhere and I adopted this idea that I was strange and weird. I kind of leaned into it and enjoyed that, although it was still ostracizing at times. I felt people didn't understand me all the time and that was sometimes lonely. But overall, I really relished the fact that I was different. Not fitting in became an asset because I wouldn't have liked the person I'd have been had I tried to fit in more or be a different "me". I wouldn't have moved to the UK; I wouldn't have taken leaps of faith. I'd be really boring, but it would have been really nice to have some encouragement, or support maybe from people who are older, someone who has gone through what I was going through. I would also say to my younger self, to trust this is who I'm supposed to be, and everything will work out. I will find my communities; I will find my passion in life. I will do what I want to do in the future; I'll be happy in myself.'

Chinelo – identifies as mixed race. Her dad was Igbo from Nigeria. Her mum is Black American.

'I would tell my younger self that you are enough. You don't need to prove to anyone who you are. You need to be proud of the times you stood up for yourself and others. It's OK to have made mistakes along the way. Always trust your gut because it will eventually lead you to some huge things.'

Natalie Evans – Identifies as Black mixed race.

'White is not the default and being called 'exotic' by men is not a compliment. Also that being seen as racially ambiguous does not detract from how I identify.'

Sophie – identifies as mixed race. Her mother is Scottish and Chinese, and her father is English and Iranian.

'Identity is fluid; you will have to and want to lean on different aspects of your identity in different spaces and at different times, and that's OK.

Your identity is one of learning and finding connections, and your experiences are valid – in their joy and in their pain.'
Anna Masing – identifies as South East Asian (SEA). She usually says that she is mixed race – white and SEA Indigenous. Her dad is Iban, an Indigenous community in Borneo, and her mother is a white New Zealander (mainly of Scottish heritage).

~

'I love you – that's what I would tell my younger self. That's what I needed to hear at every stage of my life: I love you.'
Sarah – identifies as mixed Black, and is of African American and East Coast white heritage.

Conclusion

The driving force behind writing this book has really always been what would have been helpful for our younger selves. We've often thought that many of our own struggles with our appearance, relationships and confidence have come from not having a secure sense of self. This isn't just rooted in our mixed-race identity, but we are left wondering how the last thirty years would have felt if these conversations had taken place earlier. Writing this book has been both painful and liberating. We've had to relook at moments from our past that were difficult and remained unexplored. We also feel incredibly vulnerable putting parts of ourselves out into the world that we haven't been able to verbalise before. One comfort has been the distinct commonalities between the people we interviewed who identify as mixed race and how we felt. Although we suspected this might be the case, we didn't realise just how much those commonalities would cut across people from different heritages. 'What are you?'; 'How do I identify?'; 'Where do I belong?' came up time and time again. So, if anything, writing the book has provided comfort.

We also realised how vast the mixed-race identity is and how often we would think of it in terms of being Black and white, when this is not the case. We're also beginning to understand how perhaps it's not we as mixed-race people who are confused, but rather because we think of race in such binary terms that when you can't be categorised into a distinct way it confuses other people. However, we know that there are people who are having the same internal conversations and our hope is that this book falls into the hands of those that need it.

As the mixed-race population grows, so will our need for further knowledge, discussion, resources and understanding. This book may have triggered different and even conflicting responses in you. For some, it may be the first time you have given yourself space to really reflect on your own upbringing as a mixed-race person. Perhaps you are raising mixed-race children, but have not considered some of the issues raised. You may be in an interracial relationship and were looking for ways to better understand your partner. Maybe you work with children and young people or perhaps a friend bought you a copy of this book because they want you to have more understanding of how they move through the world. Whatever your reasons for reading this book, we hope that it has given you plenty to think about, and even ways to move forward in areas you may previously have felt stuck. We are now talking about race and our lived experiences publicly in ways we have never witnessed before. We hope we will look back on this time as a pivotal moment in our history. A turning point. And to do that we have to acknowledge the importance of discussing the nuances of our racial identities and experiences.

If there's one thing we will take with us it's this: being mixed race certainly can be an interesting and complex experience but, most importantly – regardless of what anyone may dare to imply to the contrary – it is enough.

Glossary

Language changes and evolves as our understanding does. Here is a list of definitions and acronyms we have used in our writing. It is by no means exhaustive or definitive and we encourage you to continue to interrogate and scrutinise the way we use language as we continue to learn. There will not always be a consensus on the terminology we use and there are some terms that we ourselves were not completely settled on. While 'BIPOC', for example, is such a broad acronym it was our preferred alternative to 'BAME' or 'ethnic minority'. Even using the term 'mixed race' will provoke different responses. There will be a number of different ways in which people will prefer to identify and while abbreviations and acronyms can be useful, we must be mindful that we must be as specific as possible when we are talking about inequality and disparities in people's lived experience.

Ableism
Discrimination and prejudice against people with disabilities. A set of beliefs or practices that are biased and discriminate against people with disabilities.

Ally
Someone who aligns or supports a cause with another individual or group of people.

Anti-Racism Action

Actions taken against racism. In his book *How to be an Antiracist*, Ibram X. Kendi writes, 'The opposite of "racist" isn't "not racist". It is "antiracist".'[1]

Anti-racist practice will look like educating yourself through reading and taking courses, working with organisations who are working to end racism and change policy, protesting, campaigning and challenging racism when you see or hear it.

BIPOC

Black, Indigenous and People of Colour. An umbrella term that seeks to include all non-white groups.

Biracial

Another term for mixed race or multiracial, more commonly used in the United States.

Cisgender

A person who identifies as the sex they were assigned at birth.

Colourism

Prejudice or discrimination, both within and outside of a racial or ethnic group, in which people with lighter skin are treated in a superior manner compared to those with darker skin.

Colonialism

Colonialism is defined as 'control by one power over a dependent area or people.' It occurs when one nation subjugates another, conquering its population and exploiting it, often while forcing its own language and cultural values upon the Indigenous people. By 1914, a large majority of the world's nations had been colonised by Europeans at some point.[2]

Cultural appropriation

Cultural appropriation refers to the use of objects or elements of a culture in a way that doesn't respect their original meaning, give credit to the source, reinforces stereotypes or contributes to oppression. Many people have trouble differentiating between cultural appropriation and cultural appreciation. In its simplest form, appreciation is respectfully learning about another culture and seeking to connect with others cross-culturally, whereas appropriation is taking or adopting another cultural practice for the purposes of your sole benefit.[3]

For example, a fashion company takes designs or patterns from an Indigenous group for their clothing. A BIPOC may have been discriminated against for wearing their hair in a certain style but when a white person wears the same style it is considered 'on trend' and they are celebrated.

Ethnicity

This relates to groups of people classed according to common racial, national, tribal, religious, linguistic, or cultural backgrounds.[4]

Featurism

A preference or bias towards those who have features that fit with mainstream beauty standards.

Gaslighting

The term refers to a type of psychological abuse, in which the victim is made to doubt their reality. The person or organisation will sow seeds of doubt into the mind of the other person in order to retain power or control. The phrase originated from a 1938 Victorian melodrama written by British playwright, Patrick Hamilton called *Gas Light*, in which a woman is convinced by her husband that she is losing her mind. Racial gaslighting relates specifically to the psychological abuse people endure when their experiences of racism are questioned or downplayed.[5]

Institutional Racism

According to the Macpherson Report, this is:

the collective failure of an organisation to provide an appropriate and professional service to people because of their colour, culture or ethnic origin. It can be seen or detected in processes, attitudes and behaviour which amount to discrimination through unwitting prejudice, ignorance, thoughtlessness and racial stereotyping.[6]

Misogynoir

A term coined by Moya Bailey and Trudy to describe the 'specific hatred, dislike, distrust, and prejudice directed toward Black women.'[7]

Mixed Race

Individuals with parents from two or more ethnic backgrounds. The term 'mixed race' is commonly used in the UK. Other ways that mixed-race people may identify might include: biracial, multiracial, multi-ethnic and mixed.

Patois

An English-based Creole language with West African influences that is widely spoken in Jamaica.

Race

A social construct in which humans are categorised into groups based on physical and behavioural characteristics. German scientist Johann Blumenbach is often credited with creating one of the first race-based classifications. He decided on five categories: Caucasian, the white race, Mongolian, the yellow race, Malayan, the brown race, Ethiopian, the Black race, and American, the red race. The idea that the category of the 'white race' was superior based on scientific evidence was a man-made creation in order to uphold white supremacy.[8]

Racism
Discrimination and oppression of individuals or groups based on their racial categorisation. A system of prejudice executed by those with power.

Texturism
A term used to describe bias towards hair types which reflect mainstream beauty standards, for example straighter, Eurocentric hair types or looser curly hair.

White Fragility
A term coined by white education professor and diversity consultant Robin DiAngelo in her 2018 book of the same name. It refers to the common behaviours of white people when talking about race. It's a display of emotions expressed when challenged or called out about racism. It can show up in many ways, including: fear, guilt, crying, anger, shouting and more.[9]

White Privilege
This refers to the societal benefits given to those who are white. Largely attributed to Peggy McIntosh who wrote the 1988 paper, 'White Privilege and Male Privilege: A Personal Account of Coming to See Correspondences Through Work in Women's Studies'.[10] Essentially, it means there are things you don't have to consider or worry about because of the colour of your skin.

White passing or Racialised as white
When a Black, Indigenous or Person of Colour is perceived as white, usually because of the lightness of their skin, hair texture and facial

features. A problematic term, which centres whiteness and erases identity. Another term used is 'racial ambiguity' in which people are often misidentified because their racial group is not obviously identifiable.

White Tears
A term which refers to white women who use their position of privilege and weaponise their tears to inflict harm on BIPOC or avoid responsibility in a situation or conflict.

Privilege
A special right or position of superiority given to a particular group or individual.

Yellow bone
A term used in Southern America to describe light-skinned women.

White exceptionalism
The belief that, as a white person, you are an exception to racist thoughts, attitudes, or behaviours. This could be because you would never be overtly racist, have a non-white partner or children.

Resources

Professional help/support:
Black Minds Matter
https://www.blackmindsmatteruk.com/
Black Minds Matter connects Black individuals and families with free mental
   health services – by professional Black therapists to support their mental
   health.

Intermix
http://www.intermix.org.uk/homepages/homepage_default.asp
Intermix is a website for the benefit of mixed-race families, individuals and
   anyone who feels they have a multiracial identity and want to join. They
   offer a view of the mixed-race experience and a way to connect with others.

Mixed Bloom Room
https://mixedbloomroom.com/
This nine-week course is created by a mixed person for mixed people and
   centres around the unique experience of growing up mixed in a world which
   urges that a side be chosen. The main goal of this course is to create a
   thriving Mixed Bloom Room of mixed identity confidence, resilience and
   potential that can be a restarting point for any and all personal and
   professional endeavours.

People in Harmony
https://pih.org.uk/
People in Harmony was established in 1972 to promote the positive experience
   of interracial life in Britain and to challenge the racism, prejudice and
   ignorance experienced by mixed-race people, families and couples.

Podcasts:
Code Switch, with Shereen Marisol Meraji and Gene Demby
Conversations with Nova Reid (particularly Season 2 Episode 7: 'Embodying
   Anti-Racism, Perfectionism, Accountability and Love', with Nova Reid and
   Amanda Appiagyei)

Mixed Up, with Emma Slade Edmondson and Nicole Ocran
Over The Bridge Podcast
The Secrets in Us, with Georgina Lawton

Instagram accounts, platforms and websites:
@everydamndaley
@halu_halo
@Middlegroundmagazine
@mixedbloomroom
@mixedracefaces
@the.mixed.identity
@the.mixed.message
@wearemixxedup
@afrocenchix
@blackhaircareuk
@blackhairmags
@colorismhealing
@darkest.hue
@ihartericka
@mixedchicshair
@mixdhair
@unconditonedroots
@sonyareneetaylor

Websites:
https://lovejamii.com
https://www.myrunwaygroup.com
Mixed Up (online series from Metro.co.uk): https://metro.co.uk/tag/mixed-up/
www.criticalmixedracestudies.com

Books and journals (for adults):
Biracial Britain by Remi Adekoya
Brit(ish) by Afua Hirsch
Britain's 'Brown Babies': The Stories of Children Born to Black GIs and White Women in the Second World War by Lucy Bland
Brown Baby: A Memoir of Race, Family and Home by Nikesh Shukla
Crying in H Mart by Michelle Zauner
Don't Touch My Hair by Emma Dabiri
Everything I Never Told You by Celeste Ng
Good Talk: A Memoir in Conversations by Mira Jacob
Mixed Feelings: The Complex Lives of Mixed Race Britons by Yasmin Alibhai-Brown
Mixed Up: Confessions of an Interracial Couple by Alex Court and Taneka Smith

Mixed-Race Superman by Will Harris

Mixed/Other: Explorations of Multiraciality in Modern Britain by Natalie Morris

More Than Enough: Claiming Space for Who You Are (No Matter What They Say) by Elaine Welteroth

Natives: Race and Class in the Ruins of Empire by Akala

Raceless: In Search of Family, Identity, and the Truth About Where I Belong by Georgina Lawton

Raising Multiracial Children: Tools for Nurturing Identity in a Racialized World by Farzana Nayani

Sidesplitter: How To Be From Two Worlds At Once by Phil Wang

Tangled Roots: True Life Stories about Mixed Race Britain by Katy Massey

The Color of Water: A Black Man's Tribute to His White Mother by James McBride

The Space Between Black and White by Esuantsiwa Jane Goldsmith

The Vanishing Half by Brit Bennett

Wahala by Nikki May

Wish We Knew What to Say: Talking with Children About Race by Dr Pragya Agarwal

Books about colourism and light-skinned privilege:
Don't Play in the Sun by Marita Golden
Exploring Shadeism by Sharon Hurley-Hall
Shades of Difference edited by Evelyn Nakano Glenn

Books (for children and young adults):
Acceptance is My Superpower by Alicia Ortego
I Am Whole by Shola Oz and Shifa Annisa (Illustrator)
Mexican Whiteboy by Matt de la Peña
Mixed Me! by Taye Diggs and Shane W Evans (Illustrator)
My Two Grannies/My Two Grandads by Floella Benjamin and Margaret Chamberlain (Illustrator)
Pride: A Pride & Prejudice Remix by Ibi Zoboi

TV shows, films and documentaries:
Being Both
Dark Girls
Loving
Mixed-ish
Passing
Self Made: Inspired By The Life Of Madam C. J. Walker

Acknowledgements

Thank you to our wonderful editors Mireille and Marianne, the team at Square Peg (Lucie, Isobel and Maxine), Vimbai Shire, Mushens and our agent Silé for taking a chance on us. Mum, Dad, Rachel, my family and friends for their love and support. Paul and Maisie for your weekly wisdom. Robert for helping me believe I could do this. All the people who gave up their time to share their thoughts with us and be interviewed as part of the book. Everyone who has supported, championed, and shared the work on *Everyday Racism*. Ryan, Wills and Hugo – my anchors and home. And finally, to Natalie, the only person I could ever do any of this with.

Naomi

Firstly, I want to thank my wonderful family. Mum, thank you for being the most incredible role model, thank you for always wanting to do what's right by us, thank you for fighting the battles you knew we shouldn't have to. Thank you for always educating and teaching yourself and us about race and seeing the struggles we went through, even though it wasn't your lived experience. Dad, thank you for supporting us in everything we do, thank you for the wonderful memories we had in Jamaica. They are ones I will never forget. Rachel, I love you very much. I am so proud of you and who you have become. I admire your hard work and your strength. To my wonderful nephews, Logan, Wills and Hugo: I love being your auntie, you are such wonderful boys, and I am so proud of each of you. I can't wait to see you grow up and see who you become.

ACKNOWLEDGEMENTS

To all my friends: thank you for all your support while I wrote this book. Sarah, Jamie, Ali and Emily, thank you for the many dinners, coffees and support – your friendship means the world.

To Joel: I love you and I miss you and I wish you could be here to read this – I dedicate this book to you.

To Alex: thank you for the many conversations of reassurance and for the many coffees you made me during this time. I am so lucky to have you in my life and I love you so much.

To our agent Silé and our editors Mireille and Marianne, Vimbai Shire and the team at Square Peg (Maxine, Isobel, and Lucie): thank you for trusting us to write this book. What a dream team.

Finally, to Naomi, to be sisters and best friends is rare, but we are so lucky to be both. I can't believe the journey we have had so far, and I am so glad it's with you. I love you very much.

Natalie

Endnotes

Introduction

1 Jenée Desmond-Harris, '11 ways race isn't real', *Vox*, October 2014, Available at: <https://www.vox.com/2014/10/10/6943461/race-social-construct-origins-census>

Chapter 1

1 Musa Okwonga, 'The Nod: A Subtle Lowering of the Head to Another Black Person in an Overwhelmingly White Place', *Medium*, October 2014, Available at: <https://medium.com/matter/the-nod-a-subtle-lowering-of-the-head-to-another-black-person-in-an-overwhelmingly-white-place-e12bfa0f833f>

2 Cherry, K., 2020. *How Othering Contributes to Discrimination and Prejudice.* [online] Verywell Mind. Available at: <https://www.verywellmind.com/what-is-othering-5084425>

Chapter 2

1 Remi Adekoya, *Biracial Britain: A Different Way of Looking at Race* (London: Constable, 2021).

2 GOV.UK, '2011 Census', Office for National Statistics, 2011, Available at: <https://www.ons.gov.uk/census/2011census>

3 Matthew Ryder, 'What does Archie tell us about mixed-race Britain?', *Guardian*, May 2019, Available at: <https://www.theguardian.com/uk-news/2019/may/12/what-does-archie-tell-us-about-mixed-race-britain>

4 Nicholas Jones, Rachel Marks, Roberto Ramirez, Merarys Ríos-Vargas, '2020 Census Illuminates Racial and Ethnic Composition of the Country', *United States Census Bureau*, August 2021, Available at: <https://www.census.gov/library/stories/2021/08/improved race-ethnicity-measures-reveal-united-states-population-much-more-multiracial.html>

5 Kim Parker, Juliana Menasce Horowitz, Rich Morin and Mark Hugo Lopez, 'Multiracial in America: Proud, Diverse and Growing in Numbers', Pew Research Center's *Social and Demographic Trends Project*, June 2015,

Available at: <https://www.pewresearch.org/social-trends/2015/06/11/multiracial-in-america>

6 Olusoga, D., n.d. BBC – *Britain's Forgotten Slave Owners*. [online] BBC. Available at: <https://www.bbc.co.uk/programmes/articles/2XQ4ZkDRK5HGBx7Q50HPgPm/britains-forgotten-slave-owners>

7 University of Glasgow, 'Slave Codes: The Legalisation of Racialised Violence', Future Learn, May 2022, Available at: <https://www.futurelearn.com/info/courses/slavery-in-the-british-caribbean/0/steps/162113>

8 Jeff Bowersox, 'Blumenbach Classifies Humanity (1795)', Black Central Europe, 2021,Available at: <https://blackcentraleurope.com/sources/1750-1850/blumenbach-classifies-humanity/>

9 Jenée Desmond-Harris, '11 ways race isn't real', *Vox*, October 2014, Available at: <https://www.vox.com/2014/10/10/6943461/race-social-construct-origins-census>

10 Erin Blakemore, 'Race and Ethnicity: How are They Different?', *National Geographic*, February 2019, Available at <https://www.nationalgeographic.com/culture/article/race-ethnicity>

11 Martha Salhotra, 'Race Science is Not About Biology, it's About Power', *Imperial College London News*, October 2019, Available at <https://www.imperial.ac.uk/news/193488/race-science-about-biology-about-power/>

12 Morris, N., 2020. *What is 'racial gaslighting' – and why is it so damaging for people of colour?*. [online] Metro. Available at: <https://metro.co.uk/2020/06/18/what-racial-gaslighting-why-damaging-people-colour-12866409/>

13 Tripney, N., 2019. *Gaslight: the return of the play that defined toxic masculinity*. [online] Guardian. Available at: <https://www.theguardian.com/stage/2019/oct/08/victorian-melodrama-gaslight-love-island-psychological-abuse-patrick-hamilton-play-buzzword>

14 Sumiko Wilson, 'The Time For Indigenous Beauty is Now', *Coveteur*, 2021, Available at: <https://coveteur.com/indigenous-beauty-brands>

Chapter 3

1 Rebecca Gonsalves, 'Let's Stop This Offensive Term From Making A Comeback: Why Saying Half-Caste Is Offensive', *Refinery29*, March 2017, Available at: <https://www.refinery29.com/en-gb/half-caste-offensive-term>

2 Collins Dictionary.com. *half-breed*. Available at: <https://www.collinsdictionary.com/dictionary/english/half-breed>

3 Leah Donnella, '"Racial Impostor Syndrome": Here Are Your Stories', 'The Code Switch' Podcast, *NPR*, June 2017, Available at: <https://www.npr.org/sections/codeswitch/2017/06/08/462395722/racial-impostor-syndrome-here-are-your-stories?t=1632839039268>

4 Merriam-webster.com. *code-switching*. Available at: <https://www.merriam-webster.com/dictionary/code-switching>

5 BBC News, 2021. *Racial Impostor Syndrome: When you're made to feel like a fake.* [online] Available at: <https://www.bbc.co.uk/news/stories-55909105>

6 Jaynes, G., 1982. *SUIT ON RACE RECALLS LINES DRAWN UNDER SLAVERY.* [online] Nytimes.com. Available at: <https://www.nytimes.com/1982/09/30/us/suit-on-race-recalls-lines-drawn-under-slavery.html>

7 Dictionary.cambridge.org. *passing.* [online] Available at: <https://dictionary.cambridge.org/dictionary/english/passing>

8 Taylyn Washington-Harmon, 'What It Means to Be White Passing if You're BIPOC, According to Experts', *Health*, June 2021, Available at: <https://www.health.com/mind-body/health-diversity-inclusion/white-passing>

9 Isobel Lewis, '"Nobody is Gonna Kill Me Based on My Skin Colour": Halsey Admits Privilege in Being "White Passing"', *Independent*, June 2020, Available at: <https://www.independent.co.uk/arts-entertainment/music/news/halsey-white-biracial-black-lives-matter-george-floyd-protests-a9546706.html>

10 Jordan Moreau, 'Rebecca Hall on Her Family Connection to Directorial Debut "Passing"', *Variety*, October 2021, Available at: <https://variety.com/2021/scene/news/rebecca-hall-passing-netflix-mother-1235080323/>

Chapter 4

1 Williams, M., 2019. [online] Available at: <https://journals.sagepub.com/doi/pdf/10.1177/1745691619827499> [Accessed 1 March 2022].

2 Capodilupo, C., Torino, G., Bucceri, J., Nadal, K. and Esquilin, M., 2017. [online] Cpedv.org. Available at: <https://www.cpedv.org/sites/main/files/file-attachments/how_to_be_an_effective_ally-lessons_learned_microaggressions.pdf>

3 Karis Campion, '"You think you're Black?" Exploring Black mixed-race experiences of Black rejection', *Ethnic and Racial Studies*, 42:4, 1–18 (August 2019), DOI:10.1080/01419870.2019.1642503

4 BBC Worldwide, *South Korea Expert Interrupted by Children on BBC World News Goes Viral*, March 2017, Available at: <https://www.theguardian.com/media/video/2017/mar/10/bbc-correspondent-interrupted-by-his-children-live-on-air-video>

5 Ibram X. Kendi, *How to Be an Antiracist* (London: The Bodley Head, 2019).

Chapter 5

1 Lupita Nyong'o, *Sulwe*. BBC News, 2019. *Lupita Nyong'o: Colourism is the daughter of racism.* [online] Available at: <https://www.bbc.co.uk/news/entertainment-arts-49976837>

2 David Hacker (2020) 'From '20. and odd' to 10 million: the growth of the slave population in the United States, Slavery & Abolition', 41:4, 840-855, DOI: 10.1080/0144039X.2020.1755502

3 Harriet Jacobs, *Incidents in the Life of a Slave Girl*, (Boston: L. Maria Child, 1861).

4 Frederick Law Olmsted, *The Cotton Kingdom: A Traveller's Observations on Cotton and Slavery in the American Slave States* (New York: Alfred A. Knopf, 1953).

5 Kelley, Sam, *The Blue Vein Society: Class and Color Within Black America* (Bloomington: Xlibris, 2013).

6 Michael Eric Dyson, '99 problems: shades of belonging', *New York Daily News*, 2016.

7 Adamu, N., 2019. *Colonialism and the origins of skin bleaching.* [online] Wellcome Collection. Available at: <https://wellcomecollection.org/articles/XlfdHRAAAKbQ_FWB> [Accessed 1 March 2022].

8 Ramirez, R., 2020. *Beauty companies are changing skin-whitening products. But the damage of colorism runs deeper.* [online] Vox. Available at: <https://www.vox.com/first-person/2020/6/30/21308257/skin-lightening-colorism-whitening-bleaching> [Accessed 1 March 2022].

9 Godin, M., 2020. *Bollywood Stars Face Backlash for Denouncing Racism in the U.S.* [online] Time. Available at: <https://time.com/5849961/bollywood-racism-skin-whitening/>

10 Mail Online Reporter, 2019. *Jameela Jamil reveals she was 'airbrushed to have a whiter face'.* [online] Mail Online. Available at: <https://www.dailymail.co.uk/tvshowbiz/article-6556233/Jameela-Jamil-reveals-airbrushed-whiter-face-start-career.html>

11 Goldsmith, A., Darity, W. and Hamilton, D., 2007. *From Dark to Light: Skin Color and Wages Among African-Americans.* [online] researchgate. Available at: <https://www.researchgate.net/publication/23780671_From_Dark_to_Light_Skin_Color_and_Wages_Among_African-Americans> [Accessed 20 February 2022].

12 McClinton, D., 2019. *Why dark-skinned black girls like me aren't getting married.* [online] Guardian. Available at: <https://www.theguardian.com/lifeandstyle/2019/apr/08/dark-skinned-black-girls-dont-get-married>

13 Zion Market Research, 2019. *Global skin lightening products market will reach USD 8,895 million by 2024: ZION market research.* GlobeNewswire News Room. Available at: <https://www.globenewswire.com/news-release/2019/01/10/1685903/0/en/Global-Skin-Lightening-Products-Market-Will-Reach-USD-8-895-Million-By-2024-Zion-Market-Research.html>

14 Brishti Basu, 'The People Fighting "Light Skin" Bias', *BBC Future*, August 2020, Available at: <https://www.bbc.com/future/article/20200818-colourism-in-india-the-people-fighting-light-skin-bias>

15 Eberhardt, Jennifer L. et al., 'Looking Deathworthy: Perceived Stereotypicality of Black Defendants Predicts Capital-Sentencing Outcomes',

Psychological Science, vol. 17, no. 5, 2006 383–386. DOI:10.1111/j. 1467-9280.2006.01716.x

16 Bakar, F., 2019. *This is how rare it is to see dark skinned models on Vogue covers.* [online] Metro. Available at: <https://metro.co.uk/2019/04/28/ visual-data-shows-just-how-rare-dark-skinned-models-on-vogue-covers-are-9330723/>

17 Okoro, C., 2016. *Confessions of a D Girl: Colorism and Global Standards of Beauty | Chika Okoro | TEDxStanford.* [online] Secure.action.news. Available at: <https://secure.action.news/watch?v=fvoWoMlwr-g>

18 Billboard.com, 2014. *'Straight Outta Compton' Studio Distances Itself From Offensive Casting Call – Billboard.* [online] Available at: <https://www. billboard.com/music/music-news/straight-outta-compton-studio-distances-itself-from-offensive-6165173/>

19 BBC News, 2018. *Mathew Knowles: Beyonce's dad calls out music industry's 'colourism'.* [online] Available at: <https://www.bbc.co.uk/ news/entertainment-arts-42982195>

20 Imdb.com. [online] Available at: <https://www.imdb.com/title/tt0286499>

21 Vega, K., 2016. *Kanye perpetuates colorism with latest project.* [online] Golden Gate Xpress. Available at: <https://goldengatexpress.org/73291/ latest/opinion/kanye-perpetuates-colorism-with-latest-project/>

22 Adejobi, A., 2020. *Lil Wayne's daughter responds to 50 Cent's 'angry black woman' comments.* [online] Metro. Available at: <https://metro.co.uk/2020/07/08/lil-waynes-daughter-responds-angry-black-woman-comments-50-cent-interview-12963714/> [Accessed 1 March 2022].

23 Smith, S., 2010. *Did ELLE Magazine lighten "Precious" Star Gabourey Sidibe's skin in cover photo?.* [online] iMediaEthics. Available at: <https:// www.imediaethics.org/did-elle-magazine-lighten-precious-star-gabourey-sidibes-skin-in-cover-photo/> [Accessed 1 March 2022].

24 Young, Sarah, 2019. *Freida Pinto Claims L'Oreal Lightened Her Skin In Photos For 2011 Ad Campaign.*[online] Independent. Available at: <https://www.independent.co.uk/life-style/freida-pinto-loreal-skin-lightening-2011-campaign-interview-a8749841.html>

25 Donnovan, Laura, 2016. *Magazine Covers That Were Accused of Changing Skin Color.* [online] Attn. Available at: <https://archive.attn. com/stories/6579/magazines-accused-of-whitewashing-models>

26 Thompson Wanna, [@wannasworld]. November 7, 2018. *Can we start a thread and post all of the white girls cosplaying as black women on Instagram? Let's air them out because this is ALARMING.* Twitter. Available at: <https://twitter.com/WannasWorld/status/1059989652487069696?ref_src=twsrc%5Etfw>

27 Eddo-Lodge, Reni, 2018. *Reni Eddo-Lodge on The 'Blackfishing' Phenomenon.* [online] Vogue UK. Available at: <https://www.vogue.co. uk/article/blackfishing-phenomenon>

28 Morris, N., 2021. *What is 'mixed-fishing' – and why is it so damaging?*. [online] Metro. Available at: <https://metro.co.uk/2021/10/13/what-is-mixedfishing-and-why-is-it-so-damaging-15407745/>

Chapter 6

1 Reni Eddo-Lodge, *Why I'm No Longer Talking to White People About Race* (London: Bloomsbury Publishing, 2017).
2 Parker, K. et al., 2020. *Race and social connections – friends, family and neighborhoods*. Pew Research Center's Social & Demographic Trends Project. Available at: <https://www.pewresearch.org/social-trends/2015/06/11/chapter-5-race-and-social-connections-friends-family-and-neighborhoods/>
3 Alexa Lisitza, 'Mixed Race People Are Revealing Moments When Family Members Have Been Racist Toward Them, And It's Eye-Opening', *Buzzfeed*, March 2021, Available at: <https://www.buzzfeed.com/alexalisitza/mixed-race-people-racism-from-family>

Chapter 7

1 Layla F. Saad, *Me and White Supremacy: Combat Racism, Change the World, and Become a Good Ancestor* (London: Quercus Books, 2020).
2 Thompsell, A., 2019. *What Was the Prohibition of Mixed Marriages Act?*. [online] ThoughtCo. Available at: <https://www.thoughtco.com/prohibition-of-mixed-marriages-act-43464>
3 Ruth Hall, *Marie Stopes: A Biography* (London: Andre Deutsch, 1977).
4 Biography.com Editors, 2018. *Mildred Loving*. [online] Biography.com. Available at: <https://www.biography.com/activist/mildred-loving>
5 Potter-Collins, A., 2014. *2011 census analysis: What does the 2011 census tell us about inter-ethnic relationships?* 2011 Census analysis – Office for National Statistics. Available at: <https://www.ons.gov.uk/peoplepopulationandcommunity/birthsdeathsandmarriages/marriagecohabitationandcivilpartnerships/articles/whatdoesthe2011census tellusaboutinterethnicrelationships/2014-07-03>
6 Harvey, S., 2021. *Mixed up in Love*. Inner Circle. Available at: <https://about.theinnercircle.co/news/mixed-up-in-love>
7 Anon, 2021. *One in three experience racial discrimination, fetishisation, or microaggressions when dating online*. [online] Independent. Available at: https://www.independent.co.uk/life-style/love-sex/online-dating-racism-fetishisation-bumble-b1866964.html

Chapter 8

1 Ethnicity-facts-figures.service.gov.uk, 2018. *Age groups*. [online] Available at: <https://www.ethnicity-facts-figures.service.gov.uk/

uk-population-by-ethnicity/demographics/age-groups/latest#age-profile-by-ethnicity>

2 Ethnicity-facts-figures.service.gov.uk, 2021. *Adopted and looked-after children*. [online] Available at: <https://www.ethnicity-facts-figures.service.gov.uk/health/social-care/adopted-and-looked-after-children/latest>

3 Aitken, I, 2020. 'How to start talking to your kids about racism'. Available at: @everydayracism_

Chapter 9

1 Gary Chapman, *The Five Love Languages* (Chicago: Northfield Publishing, 1992).

2 Louis Chilton, 'Eamonn Holmes Apologises After Comparing Dr Zoe Williams's hair to an "Alpaca"', *Independent*, August 2021, Available at: <https://www.independent.co.uk/arts-entertainment/tv/news/eamonn-holmes-dr-zoe-hair-alpaca-b1901380.html>

3 Adeleke, Y., 2021. *The Woman Who Was Hypersexualized For The Sake Of Entertainment*. [online] Medium. Available at: <https://historyofyesterday.com/the-woman-who-was-hypersexualized-for-the-sake-of-entertainment-75e1816d0df1>

4 Bero, T., 2021. *Tangled Roots: Decoding the history of Black Hair | CBC Radio*. [online] CBC. Available at: <https://www.cbc.ca/radio/ideas/tangled-roots-decoding-the-histoy-of-black-hair-1.5891778> [Accessed 1 March 2022].

5 *Merriam-Webster Dictionary*, 'Dehumanize', Available at: <https://www.merriam-webster.com/dictionary/dehumanize>

6 Nast, C., 2020. *Who Decided Black Hair Is So Offensive Anyway?*. [online] Glamour. Available at: <https://www.glamour.com/story/black-hair-offensive-timeline>

7 Tadele, R., 2020. *Tignon law: Policing black women's hair in the 18th century*. Amplify Africa. Available at: <https://www.amplifyafrica.org/post/tignon-law-policing-black-women-s-hair-in-the-18th-century>

8 A'Lelia Bundles, *Self Made: The Life and Times of Madam C.J. Walker* (London: John Murray Press, 2020).

9 Raechele Cochran Gathers, M.D., 2018. *Hair relaxer sales falling fast: Here's why*. Medium. Available at: <https://mdhairmixtress.medium.com/hair-relaxer-sales-falling-fast-heres-why-a907ed04c926>

10 Chelsea Johnson PhD Candidate in Sociology, 2021. *Kinky, curly hair: A tool of resistance across the African Diaspora*. The Conversation. Available at: <https://theconversation.com/kinky-curly-hair-a-tool-of-resistance-across-the-african-diaspora-65692>

11 Emma Dabiri, *Don't Touch My Hair* (London: Penguin UK, 2020).

12 Anon, 2021. *The history of the hair typing system*. At Length by Prose Hair. Available at: <https://prose.com/blog/curly-hair-type-system.php>

13 Blay, Z., 2016. *Let's Talk About Colorism In The Natural Hair Community.* [online] HuffPost UK. Available at: <https://www.huffingtonpost.co.uk/entry/lets-talk-about-colorism-in-the-natural-hair-community_n_566df1dfe4b011b83a6ba4f0>

14 Virk, K., 2020. *Ruby Williams: No child with afro hair should suffer like me.* [online] BBC News. Available at: <https://www.bbc.co.uk/news/newsbeat-45521094>

15 Anon, 2016. *Do google's 'unprofessional hair' results show it is racist?* [online] Guardian. Available at: <https://www.theguardian.com/technology/2016/apr/08/does-google-unprofessional-hair-results-prove-algorithms-racist>

Glossary

1 Ibram X. Kendi, How to Be an Antiracist (London: The Bodley Head, 2019).

2 Erin Blakemore, 'What is colonialism?', *National Geographic*, February 2019, Available at: <https://www.nationalgeographic.com/culture/article/colonialism>

3 Arlin Cuncic, 'What is Cultural Appropriation?', *Verywell Mind*, August 2020, Available at: <https://www.verywellmind.com/what-is-cultural-appropriation-5070458>

4 *Merriam-Webster Dictionary*, 'Ethnicity', Available at: <https://www.merriam-webster.com/dictionary/ethnic>

5 Tripney, N., 2019. *Gaslight: the return of the play that defined toxic masculinity.* [online] Guardian. Available at: <https://www.theguardian.com/stage/2019/oct/08/victorian-melodrama-gaslight-love-island-psychological-abuse-patrick-hamilton-play-buzzword>

6 Sir William Macpherson of Cluny, *The Stephen Lawrence Inquiry: Report of an Inquiry*, February 1999, Available at: <https://assets.publishing.service.gov.uk/government/uploads/system/uploads/attachment_data/file/277111/4262.pdf>

7 Moya Bailey and Trudy, 'On Misogynoir: Citation, Erasure, and Plagiarism', *Feminist Media Studies*, 18:4, 762–768, (2018), DOI: 10.1080/14680777.2018.1447395

8 Jenée Desmond-Harris, '11 ways race isn't real', *Vox*, October 2014, Available at: <https://www.vox.com/2014/10/10/6943461/race-social-construct-origins-census>

9 Robin DiAngelo, 'White Fragility', *International Journal of Critical Pedagogy*, 3:3, 54–70, (2011), Available at: <https://libjournal.uncg.edu/ijcp/article/viewFile/249/116>

10 McIntosh, Peggy, 1989. *White Privilege: Unpacking the Invisible Knapsack.* [online] Department of Psychology at UMBC. Available at: <https://psychology.umbc.edu/files/2016/10/White-Privilege_McIntosh-1989.pdf>

penguin.co.uk/vintage